It's Your Decision

It's Your Decision

Parenting the Way God Intended

Ed Grizzle

iUniverse, Inc.
Bloomington

It's Your Decision
Parenting the Way God Intended

iUniverse books may be ordered through booksellers or by contacting:

iUniverse
1663 Liberty Drive
Bloomington, IN 47403
www.iuniverse.com
1-800-Authors (1-800-288-4677)

ISBN: 978-1-4620-3186-3 (sc)
ISBN: 978-1-4620-3188-7 (hc)
ISBN: 978-1-4620-3187-0 (e)

Printed in the United States of America

iUniverse rev. date: 06/17/2011

Acknowledgements

I wish to thank Steve and April Fritzen, the owners and operators of the Coffee Hound in Bloomington-Normal, Illinois, for allowing me to spend time at their coffee shop. Without their generosity, friendliness and support of their staff for providing a great service, I could not have written this book.

I also want to give a special thanks to Julie Megli for all the help she provided.

CONTENTS

DEDICATION

This book is dedicated to my wife, Mary L. Grizzle. She passed away Dec 21st, 2007. If it were not for Mary, I could not have written this book. When we were married over 40 years ago, I had major problems because of my home life as a child and the subsequent bad choices that I made as I grew older. Mary helped me to overcome these problems.

We raised our children to be very responsible adults. It gave me the sense that I could and should share how we lived our lives with hope in the middle of all the pain and problems this world has to offer. The most important influence in our family's lives was Jesus Christ. If God had not offered Jesus to us on the cross, neither of us could have made it to where we were when she went to be with Him. That same offer is available to everyone. All a person has to do is to accept that reality, and then turn their lives over to Christ and **"Follow Him".** After doing that, they can truly enjoy life here on earth, the way God intended.

It sounds easy but it is not. The temptations that we face daily are tremendously attractive, but we must avoid those temptations and live our lives according to what God has planned for us. The question will come up, how do we know what God's plan is for us? The answer to that question is revealed in the Bible. I truly believe that Mary and I were brought together by God and were meant to follow His guidance to live our lives according to His will.

The reason for this book is to share and help teach people what God has done for my family and can do for you if you will allow Him. Of course, it is up to each individual to allow God's will to be done in their lives. May you find the information in this book to be helpful to you in choosing the right lifestyle, the right mate and raising your children according to what God has planned for you.

I would like to make one suggestion before you start to read the book and that is to pray to God and ask for His guidance as you read.

FORWARD

It is my belief that all people are created in God's image. He loves each of us as was witnessed in the birth of Jesus Christ; His death on the cross; and His resurrection to take away all the sins of those who "**Believe in Him**" and "**Follow Him**". It is our privilege to live our lives the way we choose. God has given us choice over what we do in our lifetime. We have two choices and those are to live for God or to live for Satan. As I said, God gives us the freedom to make those choices. It is my prayer that you will make the right choice for your life. Each one of us will stand before God on judgment day and will have to answer for how we lived our lives.

We also have two choices with our own lives as well as our spouse, if we decide to get married, and, of course, our children if we decide to have them. That is to either encourage or discourage them. Discouragement is and can be a negative disaster to whoever is giving it and to the person it is given to. Encouragement is a positive to the giver as well as the receiver.

It is my prayer that each of you will indeed make the correct choices, and inherit the kingdom of God. I would like to share some scriptures from the New International Version of the Bible. They are under the heading Rules for Christian Households. You will find them in (NIV Colossians 3: 18-21.) They are as follows:

Verse 18: Wives, submit to your husbands, as is fitting in the Lord.
Verse 19: Husbands, love your wives and do not be harsh with them.
Verse 20: Children, obey your parents in everything, for this pleases the Lord.
Verse 21: Fathers, do not embitter your children, or they will become discouraged.

If these scriptures, as well as the Bible in general are followed, it will truly make a difference in your family's life. It worked for Mary and I, and our family. We were truly blessed, because we had learned the right way and that was to live for God. There is scripture that explains the importance of following God.

I want to let you know that the information in this book applies to everybody not only those who are intending marriage and raising a family. It applies to anyone who desires to live a life for Jesus Christ.

Remember: "***It's Your Decision***".

About The Author

Why was this book written? I am a man who prior to being introduced to God was on the way to Hell. So what gives me the right to write a book about parenting? I want to help parents raise their children and enjoy life as God intended. The answer to those questions follows and each of you will have to make your own decision as to whether you want to read and apply this information to your life.

I am sure you have heard that experience is the best teacher. I certainly agree, which is another reason why I have written this book. I have had over 60 years of life's experience that brought me to this point. It is my desire to share with you the reader that experience and how the problems that I went through affected my life, and how I solved them.

I started a ministry called "It's Your Decision" several years ago to try and help drug addicts, prostitutes and others who were having difficulties. I worked with several officials in the county, which included the police department as well as the county jail.

I wanted to share my personal experience over the last 35 years or so which includes riding with the police so that I could get a first-hand look at the problems that our society faces. The police officer worked with the people involved to try to figure out what happened. Believe me, it is not something that you want to go through in your family. It can be and is devastating to the kids as well as the parents. I believe that kids should never be exposed to this kind of behavior by their parents or anyone else. I worked with prostitutes, drug addicts, gang members and all other people who have been having problems with the law and had bad childhoods. I spent every Tuesday evening from 3 p.m. to 10 p.m. for four years inside the county jail in what was called the "pod."

It held 54 inmates and I was free to talk to them and could come and go as I pleased.

This was certainly a blessing from God to give me this opportunity so that I could learn first hand how the criminal mind worked. I had the opportunity to talk to men and women who had been in for crimes from Dui's all the way up to murder. It gave me an insight that I could never have found on the outside as to how and why people did the things they did.

Does this mean that all children who have had bad home lives will turn out bad? Of course not. I have worked with several people who did not have good home lives that turned out quite well. The answer for them was finding a life with God. There have been people who have turned out quite well without God's help, but I would not recommend it. That is of course, as we have said before, each person's choice.

I spent time counseling inmates and tried to find out why they were in the situation that they were. I was not too surprised to find out that the biggest percentage of them said it was how they were raised. Their parents did not do the job raising them that they should have. It proved to me that it is vitally important for parents to raise their children the proper way, and that is according to God's plan, or possibly see their children in trouble later on in life.

I had an opportunity to work in a healthcare system that took care of mentally challenged individuals. I held a Bible study and enjoyed coffee and conversation with them. I have found out that much to my surprise, several of the residents were there because of abuse in the home when they were children. Talking with them gave me another outlook on parenting and that was another effect of the abuses on children. If I had not had this experience, I would have never guessed that mental problems would be a possible outcome for a child growing up who suffered abuse.

I have included two personal stories immediately following the "Prologue." Perhaps after reading their stories, you will understand another reason why I had to write this book. Long story short, their early life was bad in many ways and God turned them around with the help of others, giving them an unbelievable story to tell. If you knew them then, and know them now, I believe you would agree.

It is a hard story to tell and read about because they lived rough lives. It appears to be a growing problem in our society and I believe with all my heart that the only solution is a true relationship with God. So if you have a stomach for the truth read on.

Even if people get into trouble, they can come back to God and have a glorious life. In other words, everybody can be saved if they truly turn their lives over to God and follow Him. Remember, God loves all of His children.

PROLOGUE . . .

The stories that follow show you what can happen if you do not spend the quality time needed to raise your children correctly, or even better, according to God's plan.

I do not want to imply that children who grow up in a bad home will break the law or become addicted to drugs or alcohol. Those who do not have the advantage of a good home life as a child will be looking for what they did not get at home somewhere else. The consequences can be very bad for your children and you as their parents.

These are only two of many cases I have dealt with over the years. They were willing and wanted to share their stories with you. The truth of the matter is, once children get into the position that they were, it is almost impossible to make a positive change without God's intervention. Believe me, they lived this. Now through God's intervention, they are leading productive lives.

The older a person gets the harder it is to change their lifestyle. It is much easier for them to go back to the old way of life because it is all they ever knew. Spending time in the jail with the inmates showed me that it is a lot easier being good or accepting Jesus while incarcerated. Most of the inmates upon release returned to their old lifestyle because they did not have a support system on the outside. This is a good reason to maintain a good relationship with your children. If they do happen to get in trouble and go to jail or prison, they need to know they can come home to a safe environment. If this happens, the child will have to be monitored and given strict rules in order to stay there.

I would like to add one major point to this prologue and that is, since God created man, it only makes sense that He wants the best for all of

His creation. He doesn't want to see His people hurting like so many are in this world. He has promised us a good life. That means that He wants all of us to enjoy living and be happy in what we do. God however, does allow us to make our own choices. If we choose not to accept and follow Him, then we are pretty much at the mercy of what the world has to offer. If we choose to accept and follow Him, He will see that we have a good life. We will still face all the problems the world has to offer, but we will have God's protection. Remember: "It's Your Decision".

Brian's Story

This is my testimony I give as a child growing up with one parent. I give this testimony to my best friend and confident Ed Grizzle for his use in his book with no intent of payment.

I was being raised in a good neighborhood, going to a good school close by. Most of the kids in the school grew up together through the school over the years. I was what some may call a geek or lame. I didn't have expensive shoes or Nike clothes, but just the normal Payless or Kmart things. I often got made fun of cause of my teeth. They had problems with an over bite. I maintained well with all the pressure up until the fourth grade and until my sisters started moving out. My father had cancer in his lungs and it was progressing extremely fast. I was not getting along good with seeing him sick all the time. Then having school kids pick on me, I had no one to tell cause he was sick. He remained sick and got worse. I got worse with worry of him dying on me at night. I often would act scared just to get in on the couch by him or in his bed so I could hear him breathing and I felt safe I wouldn't loose him. He continued to be sick and got worse. On a hot August night 1988, I was asleep in my bed. I was awakened by my oldest sister. I remember her saying "Wake up" "Come on we gotta go". I'm startled saying "what," "where we going?" Dad's not doing good. He's in the hospital, "come on we gotta go." We left to make it there just as he was getting ready to be loaded into the elevator. He looks at me and says "I love you" and his smile was gracious. He then was loaded onto the elevator and that was it. They called us to tell us he hadn't made it.

I was in shock. I didn't respond well. I had lost my best friend and only friend that was ever around. I didn't know how to mourn or even what puberty was. I was now 13 and in 6th grade. My sisters were married and gone now. It was the worst dream come true I swear. I was really lost now to a world of fear. My mother whom now I have become closer with got custody of me. I had not really been around her much. I don't really remember many memories of her and dad together. Just self memories with each. She lived in a housing authority mind you, so I moved with her. I was still lost, not mourning. I got made fun of about my clothes and teeth. My schools got changed and I lost all my school mates from kindergarten up. Things got worse. I wouldn't listen to her at all. I found ways to not go to school as she tried ways to get me out of bed for school. Her way was bribery, my way was rebellion.

Times got worse and she met a man. We moved to Mississippi. It didn't work out there. He was a violent mean man. I was in a lost world staying to myself there, scared I would get beat. We moved back a year later. We got an apartment in a fairly nice neighborhood. I was happy to be back and see grandma and my sisters and my niece. My mom enrolled me in school. I tried it a little bit but the pressure was to much. I ran to being bad as I knew not to go to school. I used pot for the first time in 9th grade. I drank for the first time about then, mind you I'm not good with dates. I was rebellious. I would have unprotected sex to move on to having kids at a young age. I wouldn't listen to her at all. I would start my life of crime now for sure. I was now staying out late at night with older crowds. Riding my bike all over seeing all things, doing drugs, drinking, sex and stealing. My mother tried as I now see, but I was just too rebellious.

Editor's Note: This story was written and submitted for publication by Brian.

Tracy's Story

"15-years-old . . . addicted to Crack-Cocaine"

Can you imagine your 15-year-old daughter addicted to one of the most "addictive" man-made substance ever made?

Well, I don't imagine it, I'm living it. Yes, that's me. I'm now 28- years-old and not only am I a crack-addict, I'm a prostitute and been to prison 3 times.

One might ask where was my parents when I was indulging in such a drug. Father being unknown. My mom gave me my 1st hit at 15. From there my addiction started. Shortly after, I followed her footsteps from being an addict to a prostitute to living a life in prison institutions.

Now being pregnant by rape, I sit again in the county jail. I am also a mother of a 4 year old & I sit here thinking of ways to break the cycle.

Parenting starts at home and coming from a broken home, I know we can start to break this cycle by teaching our children respect, communication, honesty and love. We must also show them acceptance and guidance. Help me break the cycle. I encourage you to read this book.

Once you have read this book, pray about what you have read and more importantly, put it into practice in your home especially if you have children. You will not regret it.

Editor's Note: This story was written and submitted for publication by Tracy.

CHAPTER 1: MY LIFE STORY

I would like to share with you how and why having God enter my life truly made my life worth living.

It all began when I was five years old. I had the feeling that my parents did not really care for me. The problems began when my parents abused me emotionally and physically. It then graduated to being sexually abused by a neighbor who was in high school. That is something no five year old should have to go through.

My neighbor befriended me and I accepted what he did to me because I thought he cared for me. I believed it was love because I had not experienced love before. It taught me that we all need to be loved and accepted for who we are.

I believe with all my heart, that when a baby is born, they have a heart for love and that God has instilled in each of them the ability to give and receive love. It is of course up to the parents to teach the child how to give and receive love. An important message is; "Children will do as their parents do, not necessarily what they say." This points out why it is so important that parents pay special attention to their interaction both with and around their children.

Children are watching the example their parents are setting for them more than what their parents say. I want to stress that what parents do and say are both important but what they do is the most important. Example: If dad tells his child that he shouldn't smoke cigarettes, but turns around and smokes himself, guess what kind of message has been sent? This covers most of the activities that go on in the home. In other words, if mom and dad and even older siblings can do it, younger children should also be able to do it. Remember parents, your children are watching you.

This is a situation, like many others, that children experience growing up that they may repeat with others. I felt, until I learned otherwise, that repeating my experience with others was what was expected of me since I had not been taught that it was wrong. It was showing me love so I wanted to share my love with others. Was it right? Of course not, as I learned later when I was shown the right way to live and love.

As time went by and I started growing up, I realized that my life really didn't mean a whole lot to my parents. I began smoking, drinking, and probably the worst thing was to repeat the things that were being done to me. I learned that doing these things to others was not right, because I was hurting them like those who did them to me hurt me. I was hurting others by performing sexual acts on them that were performed on me that I thought was true love until I learned the right way of doing things. I drove without a license, physically hurt other people and was indeed a person to fear. I concluded that it really did not matter what happened to me. I really did not care whether I lived or died. My parents should never have let me do these things and I believe if they had shown me the love, acceptance and discipline that I needed I would not have done them. I started to believe that my life was of no value to my parents since it appeared that nobody in my family really loved me. I was smart enough to know that I did need to be loved, accepted for who I was and disciplined. None of these things were being done at home so I decided to find a way to find the love, acceptance and discipline that I needed.

My parents did not set a good example for me and because of that, I did not listen to much of what they had to say but instead, followed the example of some of the things they did. When I talk about example, I mean that my parents did things that were not healthy for children to do. They argued a lot, my dad was physically abusive to my mom and my dad swore at us quite a bit. My dad smoked, so I figured that if he did it, I should be able to do it. I also learned how to get angry with people, also from my dad. We learn by watching others performances and deciding what will be best for ourselves. In order for me to feel accepted by my friends, I would do some of the same things they did so I would fit in. Most of these things were bad, but I did not care because I was accepted, which is what all children need.

I started to smoke when I was 10. I stole the cigarettes from my dad's dresser drawer. I started to drink when I was around 12. I began to be friends with some older kids who were able to get the alcohol. In my mind, they liked me and accepted me into their group. This was very cool for me. I got into a lot of trouble, but I did not really care because I had "friends" who cared about me, or at least I thought they did.

My parents divorced when I was 13 and that hurt me very deeply. That may seem strange because as I said my parents did not seem to care about me, but I still felt family was important. Divorce can and does destroy many people's lives. It especially hurts the children involved in the divorce.

Following my parent's divorce, I started my criminal career by committing a burglary. I did this to hurt my parents because they hurt me deeply. All I really wanted was to have them love me, accept me and discipline me. This was the beginning of my rebellion against my parents. It was my goal to hurt them like they hurt me.

Things progressed on a downward spiral. I had a woman that was brave enough to set me down when I was 14 and tell me what was right and what was wrong. The reason she set me down was that I called her a bitch and she did not like that at all. I was working at a drive-in restaurant as a curb waiter. I called her a bitch and she reached through the curb window, slapped me and told me to "get in here." I finally realized that there was someone who really cared about "me for me" and not for what I could do for them. That was a great feeling. She was the first person that was truly important to me in my life.

I did not do very well in school because I did not study or do anything to help myself. When graduation came, my shop teacher made me an offer that if I would make a screwdriver, he would pass me so I could graduate with my class. I made a screwdriver such as it was. There weren't any screws on the market that the screwdriver would fit, but being able to graduate with my class was a big boost in my life. I had a 'D' average because as I said, I really did not care. I have to admit that the 'D' my shop teacher gave me was the most important grade in my high school career. It gave me the incentive to try a little harder and showed me that he really cared about me. He was the second most important person in my life.

Between the ages of 14 through 18, I did many bad things. Things that by today's standard could have landed me in prison for the rest of my life. I committed crimes against other people that had happened to me when I was younger. I got into trouble with the law and had a juvenile record that was sealed when I became an adult. The law could seal it, but I still carried the burden in my heart and it definitely affected my self-esteem. Some of the crimes that I committed were breaking and entering, destroying people's property, and the worst was sex crimes against others. It was all the people who helped me through the difficulties, that helped bring my self-esteem up so I could start to feel better about myself.

Even after I started learning that what I was doing was wrong, I continued to commit these crimes. I often thought of the woman that helped when I was 14 and started putting some of what she tried to teach me to use. It actually helped me when I started to realize that she really did care about me and what she taught me was truly helpful. She, like with every other person, really helped me, but I had to allow the help and also I needed to help myself. I just could not depend on someone else to do it for me. Even God was not going to do it for me, because He gave me the choice, but by listening to Him, it made a miraculous change in my life. It boosted my self-esteem because I made the right decision and did not allow someone else to make it for me. I realized that I needed God in my life. I still did stupid things, but I was on the mend.

My antics brought another person into my life that cared for me. At 18, I stood before a judge and he gave me my choice. I could go to prison or the military. So how did I get myself in a position to have to make a choice like that at such a young age? As I said earlier, between fourteen and eighteen years of age, I did many things that I should not have. I did them to hurt my parents and to find out where I fit into this society. I committed burglaries, hurt people, drove without a license, became an alcoholic and was arrested on a morals charge, which was because I had sexual contact with a young girl just to name a few of the problems that I had. I chose the military and it made a real difference in my life. That was the third person in my life that cared about me.

While in the military, I started to make changes in my life. I realized that my next step could indeed be prison or death. When I went into the Army, I was still the same punk that I had been for most of my life. I thought I would run things and still do what I wanted to. Boy was I wrong. Basic training was rough but also fun. It was not until I got to my new station, in New York, that I learned the hard way about military life and life in general. I made a few negative comments to my sergeant and he took a hold of my collar, lifted me off the ground, and told me the rules. This man was smaller than I was and I realized that I was not going to get away with giving the crap I was used to giving people. After that, my military life was three of the best years of my life thus far. This was another boost to my self-esteem. I would recommend military duty to anyone who is experiencing problems getting their life in order. I would have to say that the sergeant was the fourth most important person in my life. I was convinced that God was trying to show me the right way to live.

Mary, on the other hand, was totally opposite of me. She came from a good family with five brothers and one sister. Her parents were good people. In fact, when I met them, I accepted them as my parents more than my own. Even though we went to school together, we did not associate with each other. She was involved in clubs in school and she associated with different friends. Her parents moved out of state, but she stayed here so she could go to school to become a nurse. She became a fantastic nurse, as well as, a fantastic woman. Over the years, she received so many compliments regarding her ability to do her job, and the treatment of her patients with respect and love. I never in my wildest imagination thought that I would ever meet a woman like Mary, let alone marry one.

After working one job after another, I started dating Mary. We met in a very odd situation but things worked out which I believe God had a hand in. Although we were complete opposites, it developed into a love relationship and eventually marriage. The first nine years of our marriage had many flaws on my part. I would like to share with you some of the problems that I caused in those first nine years. I had a severe gambling problem and spent a lot of time at the mobile home park office. We lived in the park so it was convenient to go play cards almost anytime that I wanted. I played poker with the owner of the business and the manager of the park. We played for big money. There were times when there was several thousand dollars on the table and on occasions, we would play all night. There were times that we would all drive to Chicago, catch a flight to Las Vegas, and spend the weekend.

The worst part of all was that I never let Mary know where I was or what I was doing. I spent time in bars drinking until I was drunk. I even ran around on Mary. As you can see, it took a long time for me to make the changes that I needed to make in my life. There were things that I did that were not very good but, Mary overlooked them and still loved me. I used to have many negative behaviors but since being with Mary, she had taught me to change them to positive behaviors. I am sharing this with you to let you know that God still loves a person even when they are bad. He does expect us to live our lives for Him, but that is still a choice every individual must make. As for me, I am glad that I made the decision to follow God. What is more amazing, is that even after all the stupid things that I did in my life, God still loved me enough to save me. My prayer is that if you are experiencing problems in your life that you will give them over to God and let Him help you through them. I guarantee you that if you put your heart into making the changes, God will be there to help you.

Mary had all the right in the world to leave me because I was not a very nice person as I shared earlier. She later told me that she knew there was something good inside of me. She encouraged me, very strongly, to go to State Farm and apply for a job. I was hesitant, but I loved Mary and believed with all my heart that she loved me, so I went and filled out an application and took the tests including a PAT (programming aptitude test). I passed both tests with very high marks and realized that I was not the stupid person that I thought I was. That was a big boost to my self-esteem, which at that time was very low. Self-esteem is a very important attribute in a person's life, because it measures their self worth and how they feel about themselves.

The higher the self-esteem, the better it is for an individual. This was the beginning of the new me. I really started to think of myself in a different light. After the first nine years and I mean rough years, we accepted Jesus Christ as our personal Lord and Savior. I accepted for the first time and Mary re-committed her life to God. Things did not magically get better, but they did get better slowly. The more time we spent in prayer and reading the Bible, the closer we got to God and each other. My wife was the fifth and most important person who cared about me, to come into my life. I soon found out what true love was. She loved me and accepted me for who I was and even disciplined me when I needed it. It felt good to me that Mary believed in me. We were married over 40 years and each year was better than the last one. We did have problems through those years, but that is normal in a growing relationship. I attribute it all to knowing Jesus as our Lord and savior because if we did not know Him, we would not have made it. I will admit that we talked about divorce three times in our marriage, but with God's help, we worked things out.

We raised two children, a boy and a girl. They are now raising their own children and doing a very fine job of it. Both families are depending on God to help them get through the troubling times and it is working for them as it worked for us. We give credit to God for the good times in our lives. We also thank God for the bad times because they help us to learn what not to do. In other words, God can and will get us through everything, if we ask Him and it is in His will. This does not mean that we will have everything we want. It does mean that we can have all that God desires for us to have according to His plan.

This brings us to the purpose of this book and that is to share with you the experiences that I have gone through in my life in order to help you to be the parent that I know you want to be. It is difficult being a parent, but with the help of God, it can be done successfully. It is my prayer that this book will be a help to you and makes being a parent the most wonderful experience you will ever have. I also want to stress that the information in this book not only applies to parents but to every person who wants to live a life for God. Children are precious gifts that God blesses us with. We must all remember that our children are our future. I often thought, over the years, how would I have turned out if my parents did their job properly. Well obviously, I cannot change the past but I can change today and that is the most important thing that I am trying to accomplish with this book. I must say that I feel good about where God and the special people in my life have brought me. I truly would not have changed one thing in my life because I believe that those years have given me the opportunity to share my life's story. I pray to God every day and thank Him for the blessings He has given me through the years. He continues to bless me every day and I am truly grateful for having Him in my life. I believe God can also change your life if you allow Him. It is and could be the best decision you will ever make in your life. I want to say that I do commit sin and do wrong, but being able to go to God and ask for forgiveness is indeed a great gift that God has given us.

I felt that it was important to share this information with you. God can and will help you through any situation if you allow Him. Prayerfully, you will find that your life will be happier and you will enjoy it more if you allow God to be a part of it.

If you choose to live your life for Christ, I must tell you that it will be difficult at first. Satan will challenge you more and more to try to change your mind. You will find that after awhile, Satan will begin to leave you alone because he will know that he cannot sway you away from God.

I would like to challenge you to find some ways that you can, on a daily basis, further your walk for Christ. A helpful hint is to use the Bible as a source to help you. I believe, from personal experience, that your day will go much better. If you have children maybe they can offer some suggestions for your family.

Chapter 2: Choosing the Right Lifestyle

It does not take much to see that our society needs help. I attribute this to the lack of awareness of us as being children of God. It seems like it is easier to follow what the world does instead of what God wants from us. That is, of course, a decision that each of us needs to make for ourselves. We usually take on the lifestyle that our parents lived, whether it was good or bad. However, when we become adults, we need to start acting like adults, and begin living like adults. (NIV 1 Corinthians 13:11) I believe we can and should live our lives the way God has planned for us, and put past behaviors behind us. In other words, we cannot say that mom or dad made us the way we are, and blame them for our actions. They definitely had an impact on our behavior as we grew, but each of us must stand up and take responsibility for our own actions. That is a tough thing to handle, and my experience over the years says that only a right relationship with Jesus Christ can provide us with the tools we need to take on that responsibility. He is the most important choice that we can make to help us to live a life that will be rewarding not only for each of us, but for our future families as well.

The first thing that I would suggest, if you have not done so, is to accept Jesus Christ as your Lord and Savior and be baptized for forgiveness of your sins. At that point, God will be with you to help you through your day. It is vital to start, on a daily basis, reading the Bible and spending time talking to God through prayer. Even though God is always with us, I believe that He will not help us unless we talk to Him through prayer and invite Him to be with us on a daily basis, and ask for forgiveness for our sins. That is the communication link that we all have with God, through reading the scripture and prayer on a daily basis.

God gave each of us the right to make our own decisions in our life. We all have free choice to live our lives as we see fit. We each must make the decision to use the tools God has given us to keep in touch with Him. That to me is, a great gift that God has given us. It is our choice to live our lives for Him. The Bible has all the information that one needs to know about living a life that will be pleasing to God. It contains information that will allow you to share the good news with others, possibly including a future spouse or your children.

Am I saying that the only way to live is to live the way God has planned for us? No. I am just saying that it is the best way to handle the life we have here on earth. Each person has to make their own choices as how to live. This book is about teaching people to live a life that will be satisfying to God, themselves and those around them.

Now that we have talked about what a person needs to live the lifestyle that they choose, how do we go about getting it done? That part is usually the hardest but the most rewarding.

First, I believe that if you want to live a happy and prosperous life, and that does not necessarily mean financially prosperous, you must align yourself with the one who created you, and that is God. He has a plan for each of his children and we are responsible for following His will to attain that plan. So how do we find out what that plan is?

I believe there are three steps to begin the process of claiming that plan. The first is acceptance of Jesus Christ as your lord and savior and repenting of your sins. One must follow Him in baptism to be raised as a new person in Christ. This will be the beginning of a new life that, if you follow Jesus, it will bring you to a much happier and more satisfying life.

Satan is likely to try to attack you and convince you that serving him is a better life. Well you can believe me, that is a pack of lies. I tried that route myself and it does not bring you anything but pain and sorrow. If you do not believe me, since you do not even know me, then just step back and take a look at what is going on around you or perhaps what is going on in your own home. I believe the obvious will appear and you will want to take a different direction in your life. Remember, life is just a whisper in time and should be lived to the fullest and to the best way possible, and that is living a life for God.

As you grow in your spiritual life, you will begin to notice that you will be happier and enjoy life more. You will obviously do some things that may not necessarily be what God would want you to do, but that is the beauty of being a Christian. God states that He is "faithful and just and will forgive us our sins". Only God knows where your heart is at any one time.

I might add that the closer you get to God, the more Satan will want to attack you. This might be a good place to say that I believe that God knows what we are thinking, what we are going to do before we do it and perhaps why we are doing it. Since God loves each of us so much, He is willing to forgive sins as long as a person is truly repentant of the sins. This does not give us a green light to continue to sin.

One of the things that I did was to step out of the forest so I could see the trees. It is amazing what can happen when you do not just follow the crowd and go the way of the world. I am sure you have heard the phrase "You can't see the forest for the trees." I can tell you that since I stepped out of the forest, I truly saw things that I did not see before. Perhaps you will too. It gives you a much better look at life and things around you. Rather than be a groupie and follow the crowd, the forest, you will be able to make clearer and better decisions about yourself and the life that you choose to live by talking things over with God though prayer.

Prayerfully, you will be able to choose the right lifestyle for yourself. Remember, God loves you and wants the best for you. Accept Him and live your life according to what He has planned for you and you will have chosen the right lifestyle for yourself. It is a decision that only you can make. With God's help, you will make the right decision.

I was very fortunate that I had a wife who I believed had to be an angel. She loved me more than I deserved and she put up with things that no person should have too, especially a spouse. She had all the right in the world to leave me, but she stayed with me even though I did a lot of dumb things. These things caused problems not only for me, but also for her. I was more like the rest of the world and followed it rather than following what God wanted for me. If it were not for Mary's love for me, I would have ended up in a place I did not want to be and that would be Hell.

I will admit that I did not choose the right lifestyle for myself and that is one of the main reasons for this chapter in the book. I chose to live my life for Satan and did many things that God did not approve. I do believe with all my heart that God put Mary and I together for His purpose. I have seen God work in many people's lives over the years. Like with Mary and I, it was up to us to make it work with His help. Even though I made some wrong and bad decisions in my teens through my late twenties, it proved to me that if we allow God to work in our lives and follow what He has planned for us, we could live the right lifestyle.

Without a doubt, if it were not for God putting Mary into my life, I would be either dead or in prison today. I guess I am really saying that if we make sure that God is securely in our lives, life can and will be beautiful. I am not saying it will be perfect by any means, but will be more enjoyable. I believe we must choose who we want to serve in this life, God or Satan. One cannot ride the fence because the majority of those who try will fall into Satan's camp.

The lifestyle we live will truly reflect on how we handle our children when the time comes to have them. Handling the demands of a newborn is difficult and must be dealt with in a firm but loving manner. If your lifestyle is conducive to children, you must be willing to sacrifice some of your own desires and time to take care of the needs of your child. There is nothing that warms the heart like your child wanting a hug or to be tucked into bed and given a goodnight kiss. Children demand a lot of attention so they can grow up, be healthy and happy and to make mom and dad proud of them. There is nothing as rewarding as watching your children go off on their own and live a life that is for God and that they carry that into their own families.

We have talked about the importance of lifestyle, how it can affect a marriage and the raising of children, so I want to talk a little bit about the affect of the wrong lifestyle on a child. If you go into a relationship with the wrong lifestyle, it can have a very negative effect on not only you but, your future spouse and children. Working with people for several years in a counseling position, I have had a lot of experience seeing what the wrong lifestyle has on both spouses and children. Usually those who live the wrong lifestyle are selfish, immature and not ready for the responsibility of a marriage and children. One needs to change their attitude of being selfish to being selfless. In other words, one must put the marriage and children ahead of their own needs. This will set the right atmosphere in the home as well as show the children and the spouse the respect they deserve. We will be talking about abuse of a child later on and I believe it would be appropriate to insert this piece of information in choosing the right lifestyle. If you and your intended spouse have selected the right lifestyle and agree you are right for each other; this will provide a safe haven for the children that may come in your married life. That would be a great thing because your family's happiness is vitally important as you grow together as a family. It will also help give your children the proper upbringing that they can use in their own lives. That would be following what God wants from us. Our God is the most giving of His love and acceptance. He is also ready to discipline us if needed.

The bottom line is, when we are ready to get our lifestyle where it needs to be, we do it properly. We need to figure out what we want in our life and how to go about getting it. We don't necessarily need to add a spouse and children to the equation but we do need to keep that in mind. They will likely come into the picture one day down the road. It is important that we decide how we want to live our life, how we want to affect our spouse and most importantly how we are going to raise our children. Once we have this figured out then it is time to start seeking out what we will be doing in the future.

There is no question that getting your lifestyle set in the right direction is a good thing. There will also be challenges over the days and years, but you need to address these issues and meet the challenge not only for yourself but, for your family. One thing that we should know and that is we only have today to be concerned about. Yesterday is gone and we may not have tomorrow.

Self-esteem is a very important aspect of life that needs to be addressed almost on a daily basis. What do we think of ourselves? Are there any changes that need to be made in my life to build up my self-esteem? I believe that keeping in contact with God is the best way to handle all aspects of our life.

Each of us needs to make up our own mind as to how we want to live the life that God gave us. If we do choose the right lifestyle and live our lives according to what God tells us in the Bible, we will be happier and will make a better life for ourselves as well as those around us.

Perhaps you can think of some things that you could do to make your life better for your future and your future family if you choose to have one. Include your special friend to help you. It could affect your relationship.

Chapter 3: Choosing the Right Mate.

I would like to share a little about when my wife Mary and I first met. We both attended the same high school but we were like oil and water. We did not mix in any way, shape or form. When we had our first date a few years after graduation, it appeared that it was a match made in heaven. The reason I say that is that my dad had a college student living at our house who worked at a local hospital where Mary worked as an RN. He had a problem because he came home and said that he had a date and no car and I had a car and no date. Well, you guessed it, he fixed me up with Mary and we, since I had a car, went on a double date. After that, Mary and I dated for a while and then, after a couple of years or so, and getting to know each other better, we felt that it was the best thing for us to marry and live our lives together. We had lived through many problems by this time and we believed that God put us together; because, as I have said before, we were like oil and water. We just did not mix. It took a long time for us to become close enough to where we could think about getting married let alone having children. We truly believed that we needed to know each other as well as we possibly could.

If our relationship was shaky; and it was, imagine what would have resulted if we would have brought children into the world at that time. I have seen first hand what bringing children into the world to a person or couple, that is not ready for them. Mom and dad need to be ready for children before having them. When I said that I have seen first hand,

I mean I have seen kids that came from a home that was not ready for them and obviously, the parents were not ready for each other. When the parents are not ready, it can cause all kinds of problems for the children as well as the parents. Raising children requires a mom and a dad that work together and have the "Agape" love for each other and the children. If mom and dad are not the right mates, that will show up in the raising of the children. As we have said before, kids will do as the parents do, not necessarily what they say. This is another reason that selecting the right mate is so vitally important.

When I said that Mary and I were like oil and water, I was referring to the fact that Mary was the good person and I was the bad person. If we had not worked on our lives together prior to children, it would have been miserable for all of us including the children. It was not until we both accepted Jesus Christ as our Lord and Savior that things started to go the right way. This proved to Mary and me that if we let God do His work within us, things will work out for the best. We both believed that God brought us together and can bring others together if they allow Him to. There is no one that has gone beyond redemption if they are truly ready to give their lives to God.

I want to address the issue of Mary and I getting together and having the first nine years of our marriage being so rough. How does this fit into choosing the right mate? Well there are exceptions to all rules and we were one of the exceptions that worked because of our relationship with God. It really is very unusual for a relationship like Mary and I had to work considering what we went through in the early years. I also believe that God allowed our meeting and subsequent marriage to teach us how to do things the right way. I believe this was the challenge that I needed to share my experiences with you and write this book. I also believe that God has been preparing me for this challenge for the last 60 years.

We spent five years together, to get to the point of having children, because we needed to work through our problems. We struggled with my behavior for two years after we had our first child. I did the best to keep my problems hidden from our daughter and continued to work on correcting them. I was the problem child in our marriage. Mary truly loved me because she put up with all of the problems that I caused in our marriage. She was a rare and exceptional person. You may be asking, why did they get married, when they were so opposite? The answer to that is we were that rare exception to the rule. I put this in to illustrate from a real situation that it can be done, if we allow God to work in our lives. Does this mean that all marriages such as ours succeeded? Definitely not. Ours, I believe with all my heart, was allowed by God to show that it can be done. It takes a lot of work on both parties in a relationship to make it truly work. Anything is possible when we allow God to work in our lives.

So, you want to be a parent. It is my opinion that being a parent is one of, if not the most, enjoyable role we as human beings can have. After all, God created man and woman in His own image and God created children in His image through a man and a woman. Now I ask you what more proof do we need. Obviously, you do not just jump in, have a child, and know what to do. After all, there is no guidebook that comes with the baby, **or is there???** (Continue reading and you will find the answer).

The first and most important thing that a person needs to do is find the one they wish to spend the rest of their life with. That can be difficult, but with God's help, you will be able to prepare yourself, and then choose your lifetime partner wisely. You just need to have faith and let God do His part.

I would like to address some very important issues we need to deal with prior to becoming mates and eventually parents.

First, both parties must truly love each other. I do not mean the way the world looks at love, but true agape love. Agape love is the love that Jesus has for each of us. It is love that says, I love and accept you for who you are no matter what. The marriage vows reflect this in the words of "sickness and health" and "till death due us part" which, I believe is the most important part of the vows. That means that each of us needs to say these vows, being truly sincere about them, and then follow through. Is it easy? Certainly not, but it is the best in the end. I believe it is really what God wants and expects from His children. When Mary got ill, discussed in this book, I was truly amazed, but not shocked, to see the amount of men who seemed to forget about the "sickness and health" part of the vows.

I saw them walk out of the hospital rooms and leave their ill wife there. I want you to know that I stayed with Mary for eighteen years while she was ill, and those were some of the best years of our 43 years together. I say this not to make me look good, but to share how allowing God to work in your life makes a tremendous difference on how you view things.

Before a marriage takes place, I believe that both people need to know each other and have an understanding of what expectations each has of the other. If you know these things, you will have a better marriage and a stronger one because you will know more about what each other expects from the marriage and each other.

Mary and I had expectations of each other and none of them were unattainable. They were not always easy, but working hard to attain them was a good thing. You have to work together to set goals. In order to work as a team in the marriage, both individuals must know what the goals are.

Is it easy? Of course not. The closer you get to God and each other, the more Satan will try to tear you apart. I believe one of the goals that Satan has is to tear the family structure down. Unfortunately, he is doing a good job. This is just another reason for selecting the right mate. The main expectation that Mary had for me was to get a decent job that not only would support the family, but also let me feel good about myself. Remember, I had low expectations of myself, prior to getting married. Mary gave me the edge that I needed to find out for myself that I was really worth something and could maintain a family by working a good job that also had benefits to go with it. She also expected me to love her and our kids when they came along. That was not difficult, because she was the love of my life and we had great kids that I could not help loving.

My expectations of Mary were to continue to be the nurse she was and prepare herself to have and raise children. As I said before, she had her life together prior to our first date. I was the one that needed the work and she seen in me things that I did not know were there until I took her advice and explored the possibilities. Perhaps you have heard the phrase "behind every successful man there is a successful woman". I found that to be very true. She was behind me 100% and helped me to be successful.

Of course there is no way that you can truly know anyone, even your intended spouse, but the more you know going into the marriage, the easier it will be to grow even closer after being married. Having said that, how will you get to know that person prior to getting married?

I believe that you will want to know if the person you think you would like to spend your life with has qualities that will fit into the life that you wish to live. You will need to find out their likes and dislikes. It would be a good idea to find out what their religious thoughts are. Do they fit with yours? Will they complement your beliefs or hinder them? If two people are unequally yoked, the marriage could have many problems such as not being very happy up to even getting a divorce. These and other areas you can find out by getting to know that person by talking to each other openly and honestly. I am sure the person you intend to marry will want to do the same if they are truly interested in you as a person and potential lifelong mate.

So many problems can be eliminated prior to the wedding day by taking the time prior and during the engagement period to talk about life past, present and future. You can get to know the other persons likes and dislikes, what they like to do for fun and getting to know their identity and temperament. These are important to find out before you get married and certainly prior to having children. Since you know these things about each other, you can work on them and make any changes prior to getting married and having children. You will find that doing so will increase the success of your future family.

Speaking of having children, I also believe that a couple should wait until after they are married to engage in sex. Why should this be important you ask? Having sex prior to marriage can and does send some wrong messages to your partner. A need to be emotionally intimate is very important in a relationship prior to being sexually intimate. it can distract from the true beauty of the relationship that God wants to see in you and your partner. With the possibility of having children prior to the marriage, it creates hardships for everyone, including the child. Waiting until you are ready for children will make it easier and you will enjoy your children more because you have properly prepared for the blessed event. Obviously, you and your mate need to make the decisions in your lives for yourselves. I am speaking from experience and sharing what I have seen happen in families over the years. I believe we need to look at the child's needs prior to our own. In other words, what is best for the child should be a priority in our lives. I am sure you have seen examples of what I am talking about in children you may know. It is not a good thing to see when children are not a priority. Children deserve the best our love has to offer them.

It is vital that parents are working as a team when the children become part of their lives. In other words, if mom and dad do not do their job and care for their kids, I guarantee someone will. I guarantee you do not want your children to get their needs met on the streets or with friends that you do not approve of. I believe that is why there are so many problems facing our children today because of lack of care, proper guidance and direction from mom and dad. The children look for it and I truly believe they have a God given expectation and desire for discipline. They know what they need but do not necessarily know how to get it. That is of course where the importance of mom and dad come in, to give guidance and discipline to their children. I don't know how anybody can believe that God wants His children to suffer the way some of them are today. Remember, if you do not love and take care of your children, somebody will. Love and I mean Agape love is the key to all relationships. "I love you unconditionally and want the best possible for you. I will also be there for you to the best of my abilities." Very important words to live by for society in general, but vital in a marriage and family situation.

When I was growing up, I did not have the love, acceptance and discipline that I needed from my parents. As a result, I made bad decisions to do the wrong things, such as smoking, drinking and breaking the law. I learned from my experience so when Mary and I raised our children, they had guidelines set from the beginning, which made things easier for all of us. They knew from the start that we loved them and were willing to discipline to show that love. That didn't mean that our kids didn't test us in as many ways as they could. I was truly hurt when my parents did not care enough to show me the right way to live, did not discipline me, and basically, let me do what I wanted. Believe me, that is not what I wanted for my life and certainly did not want for my children's lives. Today I am proud of my children who are raising my grandchildren the way they were raised. They are all believers of God and actively involved in their church.

I want to make one thing clear and that is that just because you go to church does not make you a Christian. You have probably heard the saying that "just because you are standing in a garage, doesn't make you a car." The thing you need to understand prior to having children is to make sure you will truly love them and will be willing to spend the time with them that they need and want. You will not be sorry in the end. NOTE: once you find out that a child is on the way, you need to be prepared for at least an eighteen year commitment to your child.

One of the important aspects of each person's life is, to evaluate where you are and continually update what you want to do in your life. Even though you are married and raising children, you should want to continue living the life that God has given you. If God truly brought you and your spouse together, He can help keep you together as long as you follow what He has in store for you. Remember, God does have a plan for each of His children. It is, of course, up to each of us to follow His plan. God gave each of us the freedom of choice. My prayer for you is that you follow God's plan for you and your family.

Each person has a part to play in this world. Both you and your spouse have a part individually as well as collectively to live your lives and raise your children. It is not always easy, but with God's help it can be done successfully. It does take a commitment on both you and your spouse's part. The ones that will benefit from your commitment will be your children. They will also take that same commitment with them in their own lives. When you see what your children do with their lives, you will see your commitment to your spouse and children in action. This same commitment will be an example to not only your family but to your friends if they are not married at this time.

Another thought that I would like to share is about living together prior to marriage. The divorce rate in this country is somewhere around 50%. The divorce rate among couples that live together prior to marriage is around 65%. These figures are approximate. The reason I bring this up is to share with you that living together prior to marriage can be extremely damaging to the relationship and for all practical purposes will cause major problems after the marriage has occurred. Why should that be you might ask? When couples live together, it can cause friction and put pressure on both parties. It is difficult to live together and try to choose the right lifestyle and mate. Since you are together most of the time, you will not have the privacy that you need to make these decisions. I also realize that for economic reasons it is easier on the pocket book when you can share all the expenses that would normally be for one person, by two people and save a lot of money. Is it worth taking the chance? That is a decision that only you can make. I want to share my opinion on what I believe will work if you really want it to.

Well here goes. If a man and woman love each other and one day will live together in marriage, I have a suggestion that can work for you. If you both have a good friend of the same sex. You could make it work, if all parties agree. Both men and women could set up rules and guidelines that would work for them. If you can and want to you can set up rules and goals that both of you can agree on. I would base them on what God would want for you. If you can respect each other's privacy, that would be a good thing. I would recommend that each of you follow the information in the Bible to live your lives together and enjoy each others company. This could be a valuable help to all of you. You should all save money. I hope this will help you in making your decision.

It is not an easy task, but choosing the right mate for yourself, is a true blessing in disguise. Both you and your mate will be happier and will want the best for each other if you are truly compatible. I would encourage you to allow God to work in your lives at all times for the best possible results.

I would like to encourage you to think about some things that you could do that would help you in choosing your mate. It could be things such as what they do or say. You could even pay more attention to your conversations. Try it. It could give you an opportunity to work on things prior to starting a serious relationship.

Chapter 4: Planning for Children

Hopefully, and prayerfully, each of you have chosen the right lifestyle for yourself and also the right mate. If this is indeed true, then this is a promising situation to be in for the both of you.

The next step will be to get engaged and eventually get married. It is of course; very important to carry the lessons learned by each of you into this marriage, so you can work together instead of against each other. I have always believed that a good marriage is one where both parties are giving 110% to the marriage. You might think that this is overstated, but if you do this, you will find that each of you will try to please your partner and in return, that will make you feel better about yourself and you can create a life that will make you happy. Of course keeping God in the marriage is an absolute necessity to truly make it work for both of you. Only God can bring out the best in each of you. It is up to you as an individual to execute God's plan in your own life. After all, God made each one of us in His image, so if we follow Him, we can be assured of a life that will be happier and blessed. There will be challenges and disappointments in life but we must accept them and grow to meet the difficulties that we will face each and every day. As a child of God, you can avoid many of the pitfalls the world has to offer. You can then pass those values on to your children, if you decide to have them.

What would be some of the things you would need to make a decision on as to whether you will want to have kids or not? That is a very good question because if you have kids you have to make sacrifices to raise them in the proper way, the way God would want you to. Would you be willing to sacrifice the time that is needed to care for the child? Would you be willing to sacrifice having material things so your children can have the things they need? Pay special attention, that I have said, 'the things they need' and not 'the things they want'. If you give your children what they want, they will not learn what true life is all about. We all have wants but we need to be realistic and understand that our wants may make us happy, but our needs will provide a better learning tool for the rest of our lives. Our needs being met, will give us a better and truer outlook on life, as opposed to our wants.

When I was younger, I wanted a fancy car that I could not afford and did not need. As I grew up and became smarter, I realized that I could and did become very happy with a economy car. It still got me where I wanted to go, and cost a whole lot less. It was then that I came to the conclusion that I had to take care of my families needs and not necessarily our wants.

I think it is very important that I point out the hazards of not being ready or not really wanting to have children at this point in your marriage. You really need to be careful in the bedroom or wherever you engage in intimacy to avoid having a pregnancy happen. Pregnancy in a family that is not ready for children can be devastating for you and the child. There are, of course, two ways of handling this problem and they are keeping the child, or giving the child up for adoption. Let us explore these possibilities and examine how they can affect all those involved.

The first is keeping your child and trying to make a good home for the child. This will be difficult for all of you in the home because you did not want or weren't ready for children. At this point in time you may not have adequate information on raising children and that could cause problems. If you really did not want the child, you will not only ignore, but not give the proper attention that the child wants and needs. This will cause the child severe problems down the road. This is not fair to the child as well as you as parent's and certainly is not what God would want for all of you. Since you have spent the time to develop your life's together, it only makes sense that you wouldn't want to cause problems that could land you in divorce court or worse. With that being said, it would be a good idea to take extra precautions to not have a child until you are truly ready.

The second and most important, in my opinion, is adoption for children who were not planned for. My wife and I were not able to have children naturally, so we looked into adoption. I believe that adoption is God's way of giving children an opportunity to be in a family that will truly love them and give them the life they so richly deserve.

We adopted a boy and a girl both at the age of 13 days and the first statement that we made to them was "we are so glad that we adopted you". Our children were two years apart in age which worked out for us because that gave us time to get used to one before the second one came along. We would use that phrase all their upbringing so they truly knew. Our children felt loved and part of the family due to those affirmations. Only one time do I remember that my daughter made a casual statement, "that must have come from my real mom". Our kids are grown, married and raising their own families now. It is important to let the children know they are adopted because if they find out later in life it can cause problems.

I had a friend who was adopted and was going to Vietnam. That was when his parents told him he was adopted. He lost it because he had no clue as to who he was. He was on his way to serve his country. He had a great life and was ready and willing to go serve his country and his parents. He did not go to Vietnam but instead to a hospital for the mentally challenged. This was of course an isolated case but it proved to me that children need to know who they are. If you truly love the child that you are going to have, whether naturally or adopted, you will want the best for them. I believe that you should give your child every chance to succeed in this world.

Having explored the two choices of what to do about an unwanted pregnancy, each person must make the decision as to what to do with their child once they are born. It would be best if you made the decision before the child is born. Obviously, the best thing to do is avoid getting pregnant if you truly are not ready for a child.

We have discussed the decision that says your not ready for children, so now lets take a look at the decision that you believe that your lifestyle is ready to have a family. If you do believe that you are ready for a family, it is my belief that you are ready for some of the best times in your life. There will be, of course, some hard times, but if handled correctly, they will be some of the best learning times you and your children will ever experience. I might add that they will be some of the most fun times you will ever have. Let us explore some of them.

Like I have said before, I believe that God has given each child that is born, built in abilities within their heart and mind. This surely gives us as parents a good start on raising our children. This should encourage us to use the Bible and God's message to help us to raise our kids. There is an old adage that when a child reaches five years of age, their personality is formed. When they reach eleven years of age that will be a good look at what they will be. When they reach thirteen years of age that will be for all practical purposes, who they will be in their life unless major changes can be accomplished. The ages quoted above have come thru years of experience of working with kids on either side of the eight and thirteen years of age. I have seen kids get into major problems during this period that affected their entire life. I have also seen kids that overcame these age problems because mom and dad did their jobs. These age guidelines will vary of course, depending on the child. So how do we as parents address these issues?

Mary and I experienced these age separations in our own home. We took in two girls that came from a bad home and tried to give them the same benefits that our own children had. One was eight and the other one was eleven. The eight year old was the same age as our daughter and they grew to be best friends. The eleven year old at the time was the oldest of the four children. To make a long story short, the eight year old grew up to be a wonderful wife and mother. The eleven year old has had many problems in her life that she passed on to her children. It proved to us that there was something to the age thing.

I believe there are choices that each parent needs to make in raising a child. Both parents will not agree totally on all decisions, which is why parents need to first discuss how they would like to raise their child and then come to a decision as what they both feel would be best for that child. These decisions can be made before the child is born by reading the Bible and praying to God for His help. After all, we are raising His child, as well as our own. I believe, with all my heart that God does not want any of His children to suffer. Knowing that it makes sense to do the best we can in raising our children. We need to raise them the way He would raise them. With all that being said, how do we put it into practice?

You have found out that you both would like to have children and found out that you are pregnant. Now let us discuss what we do now. The first thing might be to pray that God will give you a healthy baby, and if not, that you will be able to handle whatever God gives you. Then maybe start thinking of names, if you have not already. You of course, will need to share the good news with those you want to know so they can also pray for you. After all, that is and should be the best news possible for you since you have both decided to be parents.

Preparing for the blessed event can and should be quite exciting for both of you. If you know the sex of the child, you can pick out the name for your new child and you can start decorating the room and maybe start buying clothes. Sharing these responsibilities now will make it easier to share them later. Raising a child truly requires both parents.

If you happen to split up or perhaps you've already done so, I want to reassure you that you can still raise your child well. It will be more difficult, but it can be done. I would encourage both of you to keep as close to the Bible and God as you can for the benefit of your child. If you set rules, talk about who will take care of your child at different times and spend the time loving your child, you can still have success.

Remember, children will go back and forth to each parent as they grow. One day they may need mom, and then they may change and need dad for a while. It depends on the child's age. I will encourage you to keep your child as priority number one right after God to make your life as well as your child's life as blessed as possible. If you are separated, it wouldn't hurt, for the sake of the children to occasionally spend time together as a family. It would, if you are both trying to do the best you can, help the children in their maturing process. You as parents would need to talk about it first to make sure you can do it in a grown up fashion to keep things positive for the children. I believe it would be a good idea to keep the children informed of your decisions.

As time gets closer to the birth of your child, you can practice on each other the techniques that you have been learning and that will make you better parents when your baby does arrive. I am sure by now that you realize that having this child will take up quite a bit of your time, especially to do it right. Is it a sacrifice to have a child? Absolutely, but if you do your job the way God would like to see you do it, the rewards will far outweigh anything that you can expect in your lives as parents.

The day has come for the blessed event. You go to the hospital and after a set amount of time you deliver, what I believe is the best gift a person can receive. Your child has arrived and now the fun will truly begin. The child that you have prepared for is finally here and since you have so adequately prepared yourselves, the blessed journey has begun.

Soon you will take your child home and put into practice all that you have learned over the last several months. Every day will be a blessing, although you might not think so on some days, but as you put into practice what you have learned, your child will begin testing you. Remember, God has already built in abilities within your child that will allow the child to test you. It is the responsibility of both mom and dad to show them the right way of doing things.

Many of the responsibilities of raising a child will come naturally such as giving them a bath, changing diapers and dressing them properly and of course feeding them. Giving them the proper attention is a little more difficult. A baby has three distinct cries, one for I am wet, one for I am hungry and of course one for I need attention. A parent needs to figure them out and be able to meet the need properly. After awhile, you will be able to recognize which is which and address the need, as it should be dealt with. It does not take much to see what is happening to the children in this country. They lack proper discipline, acceptance and of course love. It is my prayer that you will desire to give your children all the love, acceptance and discipline they can possibly want. If you do, you will see the results as they grow. They will be more responsible and give back to not only you but also society in general.

You may ask, why bring these things up now? It is my desire to give you all the information that I can to make your family the best that it can be. I have tried all of the things that I am passing on to you and it truly works. Mary and I had very few major problems raising our children. We did of course, have everyday problems where the kids would test us and see how much they could get away with. They were appreciative of the way we handled each situation and it made a big difference on how they turned out. We will explore the love, acceptance and discipline in other chapters also. I believe those three attributes are vitally important in everyone's life, not only children.

We have talked about many things so far that have dealt with some of the needs of the child that you are going to have and raise to be a fine young adult. Now we will explore some of the things that you will need to learn about dealing with the newest member of your family and making it a true joy for all.

First and most important, is the fact that you have elected to have this child and raise him/her to lead a very productive life and be an asset to their community. It shows that you have made, what I consider, the best decision of the two alternatives.

So what will be expected of you as a parent now that you have decided to be one? Obviously, the most important thing will be to truly love each other and not only, show that love, but share that love with your child. A child can sense more of what is going on around them than what you might imagine. If you show love, the child will pick that up. If you do not show that love, the child will also pick that up. It is your choice. You can work on the love aspect prior to the baby coming home. That way, you will be ready to greet the new addition to your lives, with all the love that you can give. Just remember that once the baby is born, you will have to realize that you are on an eighteen or more year's journey to raise that child. It can be a good or a bad journey depending on how you as parents want it to be. It is your decision. Prayerfully, you will make the best choice for your new baby.

I believe it is time to discuss what you, as a parent will need to not only learn but do, to raise your child, and make your home a happy place for all of you. During the months that you are waiting for the blessed event to take place, you can start learning how to take care of the new babies needs such as feeding, diapering, and answering their needs. Mom, if she plans to, can learn how to nurse the baby. It may seem to be perhaps silly to work on these things but if they become learned behaviors before the baby comes, you will be ahead of the game and not have to wonder what do I do now. Many of these things will be common sense, but learning them early will help you and the baby later on. If you learn about the different crying needs of a child, you will be able to meet your child's needs easier.

Suppose your child starts to cry and you recognize it as a cry because they are hungry, you will know that they need to be fed instead of working to find out what the problem is. The same goes with the cry because I am wet or I am tired. Prior knowledge of anything is better than learning after the fact. You will have plenty of things that you will learn as the baby grows, so why not take advantage of the time you have prior to the baby's arrival and learn as much as you can? It makes sense to me and hopefully it will make sense to you.

Now let us get into the tough stuff that you will need to learn prior to and will continue to learn throughout your child's life. It would be a good idea to learn about health issues that will come up such as colds, injuries that will occur whether on the playground, at home or anywhere the child will be and other things happening that you will have to deal with. What will I do if my child gets hurt, gets a cold or has other health issues? How will I deal with them? These things can be dealt with prior to the arrival. By dealing with them before the baby is born, you will be ready to deal with them afterwards.

One of the beauties of being a person of God is that He will show you the way to deal with these issues if you consult Him. That is where I believe, that many parents get into trouble, because they will try to do things on their own. That is not a bad thing, but consulting God on things that you may have questions about is a good thing, not only for you as the parent, but for your child as well. Remember, your baby is a gift of God and He wants the best for you and your child. Mary and I did the best we could to raise our children the way God wanted us to and it certainly helped. We did not have near the hassles with our kids because we followed what we believed God wanted us to do. That is where we learned that all people need love, acceptance and discipline. God also wants us to love others, we do not have to like what they do, but He wants us to accept others for who they are and discipline those that we are close to. No two people are alike, so each person must decide for themselves, what they will do with their lives.

Remember, if you do your job right, your influence on your children will override the influence that their friends may have on them. I believe that is a great thing. With God's help, that goal will be a lot easier to attain.

Children are without a doubt a true blessing. They deserve the best possible from their parents. It is essential that couples who truly want children, are ready to take the challenge, because it will not be easy. It will be a blessing only if you want it to be.

I would like to challenge each of you to take time prior to having children to think of ways that you believe will help in raising your children.

Maybe you can make a list of ways that you can reference as the children grow. Remember be consistent in all things you do for them.

CHAPTER 5: WHAT DO CHILDREN NEED?

Believe it or not, children really know who they are and what they need at an early age. Of course, their not going to be able to identify exactly what they need or want, but they will have a vague idea. They definitely want to be loved, accepted for who they are and disciplined. All three of these attributes are important in every person's life, but especially in children's lives. I believe that the most important of the three is love followed by acceptance and discipline. Love is giving a child what they need, not necessarily what they want. The love I am referring to is Agape love, the love that says I love you no matter what. If you truly love your child, you will accept them for who they are and be willing to discipline them. When a child is born, they have no choice in the matter and they are who they are. I have said it before that I believe God has built in instincts in a child that gives them a head start. It is up to the parents to accept that child for who they are. This will help build their confidence and is a major factor on how they grow up. Discipline is essential in all lives, especially children. Discipline is structure in a child's life. They need this structure to help them grow up and become responsible citizens.

Parents need to be aware of their children's needs and help them to decide how to attain their goals. I believe with all my heart that God instills wisdom into a child when they are born. For example, they have a different cry for when they are wet, when they are hungry and when they need love. Perhaps you have noticed this in children that you have been around.

So who are children? Children are a blessing from God. Each child is unique in their own way. There are no two children exactly alike, but they all have the same basic needs. Those needs are to be loved, accepted and disciplined. If these needs are not met at home, they will be met in the world that they live in. Believe me, you do not want them to get their needs met by people who have their own interests and needs in mind and not your child's. That is why we have so many young people in trouble today. That will only get worse if we as parents do not take our responsibilities seriously. Children, if we let them, can bring real joy to a family. They are our future. That should give us reason to raise them in the best way possible. That is, I believe, according to the goals that God has provided for us in the Bible.

Children are also a reflection of their parents. In most cases, they will take on some of the same attributes of their parents. The attributes are developed from genetics that are passed on to the child through the parents. My personal belief is the environment, where a child is raised and who they hang around with, plays a significant part in how a child will develop. That environment can be the neighborhood the child lives in as well as the actual home they live in. If we allow them to use these attributes to help them to decide who and what they want to be in life then we will see them succeed. I will say that you as parents need to be aware of who your children hang out with because that also plays a major part on how they will turn out. This is part of why I believe they are born with God instilled ideals. They are their own person and need the proper upbringing to develop their individual skills and their own life goals.

Who they are will change over the years. As they grow up, they will change physically of course and their ideas as to what they want to do when they go out on their own can and will change over time. This to is a reason that they need to be raised properly. They need to be able to express themselves at home as well as school and other places they may go. They need that guidance at home to help them take care of themselves when they are away from home.

Do children want all of the latest and greatest things that are available? I do not believe so. They may act like they do so they can fit in with their friends. If mom and dad do the right thing in raising them, the children will want to fit in with their parents. They, as was stated earlier, are the product of their parents and will usually follow their example. If parents want the latest and greatest, the children will follow them in their thinking. Parents need to teach their children about what they need as opposed to what they want, using themselves as examples. Each child needs to be loved, accepted and disciplined. I know that I use the terms love, acceptance and disciplined many times but that is to emphasize the importance of providing these basic needs to our children. Knowing this, it is vital that parents spend the quality time as well as quantity of time with their children. Quality time is much more valuable then quantity of time because you can accomplish much more if you are paying attention and listening to your child as opposed to just being with them.

So who are our children? It is my belief that our children are a true gift from God. They are also an extension of their parents. Now you might ask, how can that be, when so many children are adopted even from foreign countries and have no blood relation to their adoptive parents. What about children who live with only one parent? Even worse, what about the child that is kicked out of the house? Each situation that a child is put in will have an effect on their life, right or wrong. There is an old saying that I find to be very true and that is, "any fertile man or woman can be a parent, but it takes a true man or woman to be a dad or a mom." Bringing a baby into this world is the easy part, raising them is the difficult part. That is why, as we said earlier, it is vitally important that you prepare yourself to have children before you try to have them. Raising a child is difficult but can and will bring great joy to your family, if you allow it.

To raise a child, it takes a partnership between mom and dad, teaming up with God. Parents, once their baby is born, sometimes say, I wish there was a handbook to teach us how to raise our baby. Well, there is a handbook and that is the Bible. Will it tell you how to change diapers, buy clothes or things like that? No, but what it does teach you as a parent is how to raise your child in the ways of the Lord. I recommend starting each day out with reading the scriptures and praying to God to be with you and help you get through the day. It also does not hurt to let your child help you to raise themselves. By that, I mean to allow them to help you by learning how to raise children, thereby helping them to teach themselves with your guidance.

Structure, using the love, acceptance and discipline attributes and more than that, the guidance that only God can give you, will enable your child to grow up in a way that both you and your child will be happy with. It is of course essential that you as parents be consistent in how you deal with each of these attributes. A child will be confused if they do not have consistency in their life. That is the purpose of structure. If a child has structure in his life, he will know what to expect on any given day. If not then you can expect additional problems from him. Can you imagine what your life would be if you didn't have structure as far as your work and other activities that you are involved in. It would be chaotic at best. This would not be a good example for your children to see. There is a scripture in the book of James that is listed at the end of this chapter. In other words, stick to your word and to the plans you have laid out for your family. Believe me they, as well as you will appreciate it in the end.

Children need to be raised to succeed, not to fail. That might be a statement that most would think is common sense, but it is more difficult to do than you might think. It takes a lot of work to raise a child to succeed. You need to make sure that you are there for them and be willing to sacrifice your time and energy. It is not as difficult as what one may think to raise your children the right way. It will take more of your time, but as we said earlier, once you know that a child is in your future, you have to make at least an eighteen year commitment to that child. Believe me you will find it to be well worth it. They will not need all of your time, but the time they do need, you need to be prepared to give it or have a good reason why not. If you are doing something at the time, you should not be expected to drop everything, but at least explain to the child that you have something that needs to be done and you will take care of him later. That way he knows you are not just ignoring him, but will help him. Remember, if you tell him that you will have time later; make sure you give him that time. You might want to ask him what it concerns and you may find that you will decide to go ahead and take care of his need then and get back to what you were doing later. One of the most important things that a child needs is quality time. The proper amount of time will vary with each child's needs. How you spend that time will be a major factor in how the child will grow up and to help develop his self-esteem.

Another basic need that we all have, especially children, is to set goals for our lives. We as parents will need to help our children to develop their goals. As a child grows, their ideas and plans will change. A child's goals change depending on who their friends are, what they do for fun and most important how their home life is. They need direction from the ones who are supposed to love them the most and that is their parents. As you watch your children grow and see how they change, you should notice them checking you out to see not only how you are doing, but what you are doing. You will also need to be supportive of the things they decide to do. Let them decide if what they are doing is good for them or not. You as their parents should be willing to make the final decision on what your child decides they want to do. You can and should be a source of encouragement for your child in what he wants to do. Remember how we have said, children will do as their parents do, not necessarily what they say. That applies to every aspect of their lives and helps them to decide what they want to do when they grow up.

Having their parents love, acceptance and discipline will be the most important help that your child will need. Having those three attributes will give them the best opportunity to develop their talents and truly do what they want with their lives. As I have said before, God has a plan for each person and it is up to each of us to develop that plan. Our children need more help than adults to figure out what their plan is and that is one of the most important responsibilities that a parent has. Children need their parents to help them figure out who they are and what they need. I believe that it is vitally important that parents take that responsibility, because if they don't, like I have said before, your child's future may be determined by someone that you may not want them to model their life after.

It makes sense that genetically a child is connected to their parents, so one might think that the child will naturally turn out like their parents. That is probably true as far as physical makeup but not necessarily emotionally. It has been proven time and time again that environment plays a more important role in how a child will turn out compared to genetics. A child, from day one, needs to be guided along and shown the way to live their life. One of the most important things that a parent can do for their child is to listen. Yes I said listen, listen to what they have to say and make decisions on that information. Is there a difference in what a child needs and wants? Absolutely.

A child needs to have proper care such as food clothing and shelter. A child needs to have help developing their talents. If parents do not have the ability, they should seek out help for the child if this is something the child needs. This could be a great place for grandparents to get involved. Like we have said genetics ties the child to the parents but not necessarily the talents. If a child has natural abilities and has a need to explore them, the parents need to give the child all the help they need. How can parents tell the difference between needs and wants? Sometimes it can be difficult but that is why spending time with your child can be of great benefit to all of you. It will give both the child and you as parents the opportunity to find out where each one of you stand on any given issue. Once a need is discovered, all should work on developing that need. If it is a want then all need to talk about it and decide if it is truly necessary for the child to have it. Children need a daily dose of their parents to help develop their talents.

Children will by nature want many things. With computers, cell phones and the like being so prevalent today, it seems like everyone has one or all of the things mentioned. Naturally, your children would like to have these things. They will probably want the latest in fashions because their friends have them. These are just a few of the wants that children can be enticed to have. I believe that most children are not truly happy with all of these things and would trade them for mom and dad's true love and attention in a heartbeat. I also believe that since God created each of us, and we have those built in attributes that He has given us, we know that we do not have to have all the latest and greatest things. We would gladly trade all of that for the love, acceptance and discipline from our parents.

My experience has shown me that children, as well as adults, have a need to fit in to their surroundings. Obviously, if they do not feel they fit in at home, they will do whatever they need to fit in with their friends or people you may not want them to fit in with. All children are different so these changes can and will take place when a child feels they need to make them. That should give us as parents a signal that something is wrong and we need to address the issue. So many problems can be avoided if parents give their children what they need and not necessarily, what they want. When you give children what they want, you are really telling them that you do not love them. They can, believe it or not, understand that and it will show up in their actions that you may not like or approve.

Your children, whether natural or adopted, are reflections of you. As I have said before, your children will do as you do, not necessarily as you say. They will copy your actions whether good or bad. It is obvious that having your child copy good actions would be best, but it does take more work on you as a parent. My prayer is that you, as parents, want the best for your children and will be willing to do whatever it takes to accomplish that goal. You may notice that I repeat some of the needs that children have and that is on purpose. We hear and see many negative things in our society and I believe we need to have a more positive influence for our children. The best place the children can get that influence should be at home from mom and dad.

We have talked about children who live with both mom and dad in the same home. This is ideal, but sometimes, it does not work out that way. Does it affect the children? Yes it does. Does that mean a child from a broken home cannot survive in a positive manner? No, it does not. Believe it or not some couples, even if they started out positive, experience problems that they cannot work out. Even in a divorce situation, children do not necessarily have to suffer, as long as mom and dad continue to live their lives for God and their children. We do not live in a perfect world but we can make the best of it by submitting to God and living according to what He has planned for us. No matter what, the parents are the most influential people in a child's life. Without a doubt, parents have an awesome responsibility. The love, acceptance and discipline children receive from their parents, whether they are together or not, are vital to the children and they definitely need and want it. It is definitely better if parents remain together if at all possible.

So who are our children? They are a gift from God that was given to their parents to bring joy and a challenge to them. They can be the light of a parent's life, if we let them. So what do our children need? They want to be loved, accepted and disciplined by their parents. They want to be raised to be people who will contribute positively to society. They also want to be given the best that their parents can give. Remembering that our children, like ourselves, were created in the image of God and should in itself be enough to convince us that He only wants the best for all of His children.

That should also give us the desire to want the best for our children and our spouse. We should learn as much as we can about our child and do the best that we can to provide their needs. By the way, it would not hurt to throw in a little something that they want every now and then. This can be a special treat for them.

Children are a gift from God and deserve the best we have to offer to them as their parents. That does not mean material things but does mean the love and respect that they need and want. The rewards of treating our children as God treats us are immeasurable. They also need the best guidance that you can give them as they grow up and mature.

I would like to challenge you as parents to work on some ways that you can bring out the best in your children. Find ways that will help you see what they need and who they really are. This could help you in many ways while you are raising them. Believe me, your children will appreciate your attention.

James Chapter 5:12 (NIV)

Above all, my brothers, do not swear--not by heaven or by earth or by anything else. Let your "Yes" be yes, and your "No" no, or you will be condemned.

Chapter 6: The Important Years in a Child's Life

It is my belief, through experiences over the last several years, that from the day that a child is born, they have specific needs and have built in knowledge that God has given them. Some people say that a child is born with an evil heart. To me that is one of the dumbest things that I have ever heard. Since man was created in the image of God that would mean to me that God has an evil heart. That is one argument that each individual has to settle for themselves. As for me, I do not believe it for one moment. I do believe that a child's heart can become evil if their parents fail in their duties to the child. If parents do not care for their child, they will grow to not trust them and believe that they are not loved. Children can and will turn on their parents if their needs are not met. That is rebelling. I myself got into trouble with the law and did stupid things because of my parents feelings for me and how they treated me. Was it worth it? Definitely not.

I do believe that as children grow, their needs change and it is vitally important that parents pay attention to their children and learn as much as they can to help raise them in the way God intended. To learn about what God intends for his children, read the Bible and study it. You will learn more of what you may need to raise your children by doing so.

Every year in a child's life is important, but there are special years that are more important than others. Girls have more years going through puberty than boys for example. We will explore those later. We need to take into account that depending on the child's makeup, their important years will be different than others in their age range. Parents need to be aware of those important years as well as all years of their children's lives so they can be in touch with things that are going on with them. Things can change rapidly in a child's life and parents need to be aware of what is going on with them at all times. Children, like adults, need to have their privacy of course, but we also need to be aware of our children's activities so we can teach them how to stay out of trouble and encourage them to do well.

Let us begin with the first years of their life from birth to about two years old. Obviously, the first couple of years they will be starting to get used to mom and dad. They will begin to learn what they need to do to survive in their new environment. It is quite different from being in their mother's womb where everything was done for them and they were quite comfortable. They must now learn how to get their parents attention when they are hungry, need a diaper change and when they feel the need for attention. In the womb, as I said before, everything was done for them. I have said this before and will probably say it again, that God has given every child abilities that they will need to survive in this life. The first years are vital in the raising of a new child. The parents and child need to get used to each other and to the daily routines. Home life has now changed drastically for all concerned. Not only does the child need to learn but mom and dad also need to learn how to handle things with a new baby in the home. It will be a challenge for all. Now is the reason for doing the practice and learning prior to the baby's birth. I believe that if you did the pre-learning, you will appreciate it much more now.

You may want to re-visit the pre-learning once in awhile for a refresher course. My intention is not to confuse you or make things more difficult, but to help you through some of the rough times. I know that I learned a lot from those who went through it prior to Mary and I going through it. I hope to pass on some valuable experience to you so you can have an easier time with raising your own children. Each couple needs to adjust their techniques to fit their particular needs. Having said that, since we were created in the image of God, we will have some abilities built into ourselves that will truly help us get through the tough as well as the good times. We just need to keep the faith and let God lead us through those times and life itself. He will take care of us (NIV Matthew 6: 25-34)

Let us explore the important years of your child's life. We have talked about the two years after you brought your child home already. These are somewhat getting used to each other. Taking care of a baby up to two years old is mainly loving them and taking care of their needs. Now, what about the "terrible twos"? Everybody knows about them and if they have had children they have lived through them. I believe that the "terrible twos" come natural for all children. They are beginning to walk and talk better and can challenge mom and dad's authority. These years can be a major challenge for parents and is definitely a time that if parents get through it, it will seem like the years to come will be somewhat easier. That is not necessarily true. It is important for the children to adapt to parents in those first couple of years so they can, so to speak, test the waters and see how their parents will react. The following years will be just as challenging, but will be more rewarding as we see our children grow up to be successful adults. If you get through the "terrible twos", you and your child will have learned a lot about each other and will be able to move on to the next group.

Lets move on. The threes, fours and fives will be challenging and extremely important because as we have said before, a child's personality is formed around age five. This means, in my opinion, that you as parents need to pay special attention to the development of your child's interests and needs in these three years or so. Every child develops at a different rate, so if you have more than one child, each one of them will more than likely be different. So how do you go about working with your three to five year olds? It is a good idea, even at their tender years, to introduce them to the Bible stories and include them in family meetings so they can feel like a part of the family. Of course, we cannot forget the playtime that they will need. Remember, your children are a gift of God, so do not under estimate their abilities. Parents need to pay special attention to their child's likes and dislikes and how they behave around you and other people. Remember, they are forming the personalities that God gave them and they will need all the help they can get.

You can be an encourager or a discourager by your actions and how you treat them. It is up to you as to how you will help them develop the natural talents and abilities they possess. You might also pay special attention to how you as their parents behave around them because they will pick up what you are doing and use that to help develop their natural abilities. You will, if you handled it properly, see an idea of what your child's personality will be when they grow up. Your child will spend some time in pre-school and perhaps kindergarten. This will also help them since they will be around other children and seeing how they are acting. The most influential place that your child will be is in the home, whether good or bad. In other words, the child will learn more and form their personality, from what goes on in the home at an early age. This places an awesome responsibility on the parents, but the results will be wonderful if you do your job correctly.

Let us move on to the next age group and that is from six to eleven where a child will become what they will be for the most part. You have gotten them through the baby stage of their life, the "terrible twos" period and the three through five years period and if you are still sane, you have made it through what I believe are the most important years of your children's lives. If things are going well, then you have done a great job. It will be a little easier in the next age group since you did so well before and helped your child form their personality. Good job. Keep up the good work. The six to eleven age groups is very critical also. It is the time when your child needs to have the direction of who they will be as an adult. Their in school and learning all kinds of things that will help them in their future, to become the person God intended for them to become. If you give them the best you have been blessed with, they will shine at school and be a blessing to their friends. They will begin to try to mix fun with training and thinking about who they want to be and what they might want to do. It is important that you help them by spending time with them, not only having fun, but listening to them and helping them with their needs.

Throughout all of the years with your child, you need to listen to them and help them with their questions. If you do not, believe me, someone that you do not want to help them will be there for them. The outcome may not be what you want. It is of course, your choice. This age group will be exploring different options and ways they can learn how to find themselves. This will help them to discover who they are and what they want to be. Obviously, it is a parents' obligation to help their children by meeting their needs. Spending time with them, even though they might fight it at times, will be good for all concerned.

There will be a lot more testing in this age group. Because your children are growing up and trying to identify who they really are, they will explore the limits just to see what you will do and how you will handle them. Remember, we talked about that who your child is at age eleven, for all practical purposes will be what your child will be unless major changes take place. That is why I believe it is crucial that you as parents take the responsibility that God has given you to love, accept and discipline your children. Just a note at this time and that is that God doesn't want any of His children to suffer in anyway. He wants the best for all of us but He has given us the responsibility to make the decision for our own lives as well as our children as they are growing up.

The next group is age twelve through fifteen. These will be probably some of the hardest years for the children and could be hard for you as their parents. Your children, when they get in this bracket, will be experiencing physical changes to their bodies as well as their minds. They will be in between children and young adults. It is an awkward age group and this is when they will need all the encouragement they can get from mom and dad. I believe since your children are growing up and going through puberty, they will need all the help they can get to get through it. Believe me, it is better that they find out the truth at home, rather than on the streets.

Kids in this age group are experimenting with these new feelings. If you as their parents are willing to take the time to spend with them and answer questions that they may have honestly, you will help your children immensely. It is definitely better that the children learn at home in a safe environment than elsewhere. With the changes will come questions. Those questions will sometimes be hard to answer and think about, but the answers will need to be truthful and to the point. Typically called "the birds and the bees". Teach them right and they will grow up appreciating you and all that you do for them. They will love and trust you more if you are honest with them on all subjects. Remember, once a child reaches thirteen, that will more than likely be what they will be in their life unless a major change takes place. That is why it is critical all the years of raising a child that they be given the love, acceptance and discipline that they need and want. If you have raised your child well and according to God's plan, they will not need a major change in their life.

The next group will be sixteen to nineteen. These will be the high school years for all practical purposes and will be difficult but not impossible. This is when young people want to prove who they are to anybody who will listen. They will want to date and go to parties. They will also want to hang around with their friends. That is great as long as their activities are monitored. I believe that this is one of the toughest times for a child because they are truly finding out where they fit into society and will truly be putting you as parents through the hardest tests that you will need to pass. They will want to do as their friends do and that can be a problem. This is the time they may be thinking of what will they do after high school and before they go out on their own. They will need all the support and help they can get from mom and dad. They will have a great need for approval and love that only you as a parent can give. Be sure to be ready to answer questions, discipline them and love them. They will need all of the above now more than ever. If you have gained their respect and trust over the years, they will need and appreciate you even more through this age group.

When a child goes off to college or out to live on their own, it is vital that they have the knowledge that they will be welcome home at any time. That is a wonderful feeling that you can send your children off with. You can then realize that you have done a great job over the years and be truly proud of your children. You will find that all the hard work, love, acceptance and discipline that you put into your children will be well worth it. I also truly believe that if you have had problems with your children and they leave for various reasons, you should keep the "open door" policy available to them. In my years, I have seen parents who close the doors on their children and have regretted it later on. Unfortunately, it may very well be too late and your child may have ruined their life. I don't believe that any parent would want to see their child ruin their life.

There will come a time, hopefully not for you that a child will be lost to the world and you cannot do anything about it. The best thing is to take care of the problem before it becomes one and raise your children according to what God has planned for you. I have also seen parents who have kept the doors open for their children on unconditional terms and were glad they did. Like I have said before, the home is the most influential place your child will ever be. If they know that in their hearts, it can make a great difference in how they act and feel about you as their parents.

I would like to take a couple of minutes to share with you the importance of starting your life with God and raising your children in the ways that God would like you to. If you do, you will truly enjoy your life to the fullest as will your family. God created each of us in his image and He loves us and truly wants the best for each of us. He does have one desire and that is that we truly love Him and follow Him. Of course, that is the decision of each individual. You as parents are responsible to teach your children about God and how to live according to His will. The results will be that you will have a wonderful life. You will still have some problems, but God can see you through them if you allow Him.

All years are important for a child. It does take a lifetime to raise a child and it takes dedicated parents. As we have said before, everybody needs love, acceptance and discipline, especially children as they are growing up. With the help of God, the job of raising a child can and will be more fun and more enjoyable. I hope that this information will help you to get your child through the different age groups successfully.

I would like to challenge you to come up with ways that can make all the age groups the best they can be. Maybe you can make up a schedule that will help you make things work out the best for all of you.

Chapter 7: Be Completely Honest With Your Children

It is my hope and prayer that the message in this book will indeed help you in raising your children the way God would like to see them raised. That is one of the best ways a parent can honor God by raising His children in the right ways. The Bible mentions some scriptures that you might want to read and see that God does truly love all of His children. Do you remember that we mentioned the guide book in chapter 2? Well, I believe the Bible is the guidebook, to show us how to raise our children. In fact, I believe that the Bible is the guidebook to live our lives to the fullest. Not all families have the same situation in their homes because people are different and look at things differently; therefore, they need to interpret the information in the Bible according to their families needs. I want to clarify that the Bible does not change, but since people are at different levels in their walk with God, the same set of scriptures can and will mean something different to each of them. I am convinced that the Bible can and will help you as parents to not only live your lives as God wishes for you, but also to raise your children up in the same way that God wants you to. You will definitely not be sorry for using God's way to living life with your children and your spouse.

Being completely honest with your children is an awesome responsibility that parents have in raising their children. Honesty requires being totally truthful in everything you do, not just as parents. Your children need to see that truth in you before they will truly trust you. Trust is an attribute that needs to be earned and is one of the most important attributes in a marriage let alone when raising children. You can be honest in several things and gain the respect and trust of your children, but lose it on just one thing that is not truthful. So you can see the importance of being completely honest with them. Just like the statement that you tell your child that "you are a good boy" one hundred times and tell him that "he is a bad boy" just once, he will accept and believe that he is a bad boy. I do not believe that you as a parent would really want that.

As children grow and mature, they will have more questions to ask and hopefully, you as a parent will have the trust of your child so they can come to you for the answers they need, not necessarily want. This I have also said before, and will probably say again, and that is if you do not take care of your child's needs at home, somebody out there will. You may not like the answers they will get, so for your families sake, be completely honest with your children.

Your children will pick up your habits quickly because they will do what you do not necessarily what you say. This is another major reason for being honest with your children. Remember, they are smarter than what you give them credit for. That is not a put down to you as a parent, but sometimes children hide feelings very well. I believe that is for a reason and that is they are always testing you. Does it take more time to be honest with your children? Sometimes it will, but the results that you get, will be well worth the time that you spend. You will gain your child's trust and respect when you are completely honest with them. Some say that you need to be careful how you answer your child's questions because it may hurt them. That is true at times, but would you rather hurt them with the truth or a lie? Children for the most part will be hurt at times when they have their questions answered, but it is always best to be truthful rather than tell a lie. Remember, each parent has to make that decision for their own family. When you tell one lie and one hundred truths, a child is more apt to believe the one lie over the truths. I cannot answer why that is, but in my experience, it seems to ring true. It is not something that I would recommend testing.

So when does telling the truth to your child begin? I recommend starting from the day they are born. Mary and I adopted our children at the age of 13 days and on the way home, we kept saying to them, "we are so happy that we adopted you". Bottom line is that over the years they never had any questions about where they came from. They knew we were their parents and that they were adopted. Only once in their life was anything said and that was by our daughter when one day we left the house and she did something, I don't remember what, but she said "I must have got that from my real mom". That was the proof that we needed to know that we had to be very truthful with them all the time. Did we goof occasionally? Of course we did, because we are not perfect and like everybody else, we were subject to making mistakes. Do we regret being very honest with our children? Certainly not. Otherwise, I could not recommend this to anyone with true honesty.

Are there any times that we do not want to be honest with our children? I personally do not believe so. I do believe that there are certain questions that may be asked by our children that we might want to wait to give them the full answer. In other words, the truth needs to be age sensitive. We were completely honest with our children and they not only appreciated it, but carried that same honesty into their marriage and family. It does, like everything else, flows down through the generations of a family.

I do want to touch on what can happen if parents are not completely honest with their children. The first and what I believe is the most important is the children's lack of trust for their parents. If a child cannot trust their parents, they will find trust in someone else. There again, that trust in someone else may not be in the best interest of your child. Remember, we said earlier, that if parents do not do their job at home, a child will find someone who will. Trust is vital in all relationships especially parent to child.

I want to take a little time now to address another issue and that is to make sure that you teach your children at an early age about strangers or any one else that could cause harm to them. Children are very vulnerable at any age but especially in the earlier years. I have a little girl about six or seven that lives next door to me and she is extremely friendly. She came to my door with her little friend just to say "hi". They trusted me but what could have happened if there was a not so trusting man at the door. What I am saying is that all people are not trustworthy and should not be around children. I believe with all my heart that we must teach our children about what to do in a situation involving someone they do not know or do not know very well. You never know what can happen, so please be careful with your children. I believe children are born with trusting hearts and need to be nurtured in truth. Be sure to watch your kids when you are out in public with them. Watch who they are with and who is around them. This could be an important subject to discuss in your weekly family meetings.

We talk about importance of grandparents in a later chapter. The relationship between grandparents and grandchildren is one of the most important relationships next to parent and child. If a child cannot trust their parents, they may very well find that needed trust in their grandparents or other members of their family. That would be far better than finding it on the streets, where so many do find it. Trust is vital, but so are love, acceptance and discipline. Believe it or not, truth does effect love, acceptance and discipline more than you might imagine. If you tell your child you love them and then lie to them, what are you really telling them? Certainly, that does not show love. If you tell your child that, you accept them for who they are and lie to them, what are your really telling them? That also does not show that you accept them for who they are. If you discipline your child and are not consistent with it, you are really lying to them because you are saying to them that discipline is not important. There again you are actually lying to them.

Everything actually ties back to choosing the right lifestyle, and the right mate. Will your new lifestyle together want children? It is an awesome responsibility to raise children. I am convinced that if we follow what God has planned for us, we will certainly have a fulfilling life with or without children.

I employ you to be totally honest with your children and raise them according to the plan that God has for you. If you do, you will be extremely happy about the decisions that you make. Not all decisions will be completely right, but if prayer to God precedes them, they will turn out for the best in the end. I do not want to say that life will be easy because it is not. If it were, it would not give us a chance to use our faith in God to help us each day.

Being honest with your whole family, especially children, will make a real difference in everybody's life. If children are raised to respect and tell the truth, they will have a better life and so will you.

I would like to challenge you as parents to come up with ways that you can keep truth as one of the most important attributes in your home. Come up with ways that you can teach your children about truth and the importance of it.

Chapter 8: Our 43 Years of Married Life

I want to share our married life with you because we experienced a wide range of problems in our lives prior to accepting Jesus Christ and following what He wanted for us. I need to say that I loved Mary more than life itself.

Mary and I were married in 1965 at the age of 24. As I said in my story, which you would have already read, my life as a child through my late 20's was not a life that was worth very much. I did not think very much of myself during that period. Mary and I went to the same school but at that time neither one of us ever thought of each other as a friend let alone a spouse years later. We met officially when a friend who was staying at my dad's house worked at the hospital that Mary worked at. He came to me one day and said he had a date and no car. He also said that I had a car and no date. He said that he would get me a date and since I had the car, we could double date. As you may have guessed, it was Mary. That began a beautiful relationship that lasted for over forty years.

Our first nine years were tenuous at best. I did not do things the way I should have as a husband and still she stayed with me. I went from one job to another and one day Mary made me go to State Farm because some of her family was working there at the time and obviously, she had faith that I could also make it work for me. I took the test and it made me sit up and take notice that I was not dumb like I thought and that I was of some value. I began to see what Mary saw in me. Perhaps I was worth something and worth saving.

For the first five years, we planned to try to have a child without success. We decided to look into adoption because we thought we were ready for kids and within two years, our dreams were fulfilled. We adopted our first child, a daughter, when she was 13 days old. That was the start of another chapter in our lives. We found out that raising children and having both parents working was not as easy as we thought. We made a commitment to our daughter and that was to spend time with her. It did not take long to find out that having children was fun and a lot of work, but definitely well worth it. Within two years, we adopted our son. He too was a joy to have around. It doubled our work but was truly worth it.

We were still having problems in our marriage but we were working it out as best we could at the time. We both believed that our children were the most important members of our family and they deserved the best we could offer.

We had good friends that were our neighbors. They invited us to go to their church, so we did. That was my first true look at Jesus Christ. I went to church as a kid but that did not mean much to me because my family did not care very much for me and never taught me that church was important. Therefore, I did not think much of myself either. Now things were different because I had a woman and two children that truly loved me. I believe I truly felt what true love was for the first time in my life. Others down through the years loved me, but not like my family.

One day, our friends invited us to their home to attend a Bible study, and it was a study on Revelations. I must say it really scared me to think that I was going to hell if I did not change my ways. It was my awakening to truly find God and invite Him into my life. I realized that I needed Him in order to live my life according to His will. With that in mind, Mary and I decided that we needed to make changes in our lives in order to raise our kids according to what God would have wanted us to do. Mary and I decided that we were ready to accept and be baptized into Jesus Christ. We talked to our minister and decided to do it on Easter Sunday of 1974. The minister came back to where we were sitting and told us that we might want to wait, because the baptistery was off and the water was cold. We told him that we were ready now and went forward to be baptized into Jesus

Christ. Mary and I both felt that if we decided to wait, our hearts were not truly into accepting Jesus. We decided that we were going to follow the Bible and Jesus to the best of our abilities. Nobody said it would be easy, but it was truly worth it in the end. It is not an overnight transformation and it does take time because Satan is always trying to tempt you into doing something that God would not want you to do.

We both noticed a difference in our attitudes, how we felt about each other and those around us. The children became the highlight of our lives and we spent the time raising them, as God wanted us to. Of course, we both made mistakes but in the end, our children were happy and had a good childhood. I would like to say something about when both husband and wife work. Mary and I did it and still managed quite well raising our children. I believe that if you are in that situation, you to will handle it quite well.

Over the next several years, things continued to get better, but of course there were challenges. Mary took ill in 1990 losing her kidney and having to spend the month of January in the hospital. We came close to losing her then and three other times prior to her passing in December of 2007. We had asked a woman from our church to answer the business phone for us since we both worked at the time. She continued to answer the phone since I was caring for Mary. She was very instrumental in our lives because she was the drop off point for food cooked by different friends from our church. I would stop and pick up the food and take it home to Mary. She also had a boy and a girl who were twins about eight years old when I met them and since she had been divorced, I helped her with the kids. I took them places like swimming and fishing to mention a couple. This family became very important to my family during Mary's illness and will not be forgotten. The boy is now a campus minister at a college campus and the girl is working in town after coming back from Florida. I praise God for all three of them. They helped me get through the next several years of Mary's illness. I do have to admit that I made a mistake with the girl because when she turned thirteen, I had to leave to take care of things at home. I learned later that I hurt her because later when I finally went back to her, she told me that she really needed me and I was not there for her. That convinced me that we needed to be more careful with raising our children than I thought at that time. Kids will need their father and mother at different times in their lives. This was the time that I was needed and I let her down. It proved to me that girls need their fathers or at least a good male role model when they start going through puberty.

I mention three other times that Mary could have passed but God still had a purpose for her and He kept her around for a total of eighteen years. It was tough going through those years, but with the help of the kids and the rest of the family, it was great and we could not have done it without them. I believe that the only way our family stayed together was because of our faith and belief in God.

As I said earlier, being a Christian is not easy because we are always subject to sinning. Most of the sins that we committed were ones that looked very attractive and were indeed fun. The greatest thing was that we could go to God through Jesus Christ and ask for forgiveness of our sins. I must add that being human is not an excuse for sinning. I am sure you have all heard or used yourself the phrase that 'I am only human' when committing a sin. In my opinion, that phrase does not hold water.

The last eighteen years of our marriage had its difficulties but we depended on God to get us through and I must admit that He did a great job helping us through those tough years. If it were not for Him, we would have never made it. I am touching on these eighteen years because they were important growing years for not only me, but also our children. It truly showed us that by depending on God, we could get through anything. I must say that we had some bad times as well as good times during the period that Mary was ill. Maybe you will remember that I said that God would see you through the good times as well as the bad times. Believe me it is true. We just have to put our faith in Him and follow what He has in store for us. Mary and I did, the best we could, and even the children did a wonderful job accepting what was going on and how they fit into the picture. I certainly pray that you will not have to go through difficulties like extended illness or any other turmoil in your family. Believe me, it is only as bad as you let it be, but you need to follow the vows as we said before and do the best that you can to keep the family together. Having God to help will make all the difference in the world.

Mary did extremely well handling things such as Dialysis, going to the hospital various times and just the everyday problems that existed for her. I was very pleased with the children because they did a great job helping in many ways. This made a difference in how we reacted to each other in the family. We all had good days and bad days, but we got through it because of our faith in God. If we truly follow God, He will not let us down. We have talked about the importance of having family meetings to talk about what is going on in the home and with each person in the family. This gives everybody a chance to get their views on the table and discuss them as a family. Mary and I did that early on in her illness and it made a world of difference on accepting the reality of her passing one day. In our family meetings, we all got together and discussed not only Mary's illness but also all the other things that were going on with the children and myself. As I said before, it was wonderful how it affected the family. Truth and honesty will win out every time. It is my opinion, that keeping the family up to date on important things going on, will increase trust and respect for each other.

I want to share a little about the eighteen years that Mary was ill. Even though she was ill, she did not let it show. Most people who did not know us would have never known because she did not show that she was ill. She was what I called a trooper when it came to her faith in God and trying not to harp on her illness and the negative but to share the positive things that were going on. I can only hope and pray that if I get that ill that I can follow her example. Very few people really knew how ill she was. She had two close friends that she kept in contact with and both of them knew her well. Mary and I spent a lot of time over the last three years of her illness playing rummy and just keeping each other company and encouraging each other. We grew to learn a lot more about each other during that time. We played several games of rummy in the last two weeks of her life. It came down to the last day and a half that she started to fail that she went to sleep and never woke up. I do want to mention that Hospice was there for the last 16 days of her life and did a fantastic job of taking care of her and keeping her comfortable until the end.

Another aspect that was vitally important for our family was setting up final arrangements, not only for Mary, but also for me. We had medicine lists for both of us. It became very important because Mary got to the point that she had to have her meds given to her. Had I not known nor had the list, that could have presented a major problem. You might want to know, why is this important in a parenting book? Well the answer to that is that it falls under parenting because children need to be kept in the loop about all things that are going on in the home. Does that make sense? I hope so.

When the end got very close, we called Hospice in to help take care of her needs. We had a family meeting during this time and informed everyone of what we were going to do and that it was getting close to time for Mary to go home and be with God.

The children as well as I were very appreciative of that meeting because it gave us the information that we all needed to be ready for Mary's passing. We celebrated Christmas with our whole family and that was on December 15. It was an awesome Christmas, because mom was there with us. As was in the Dedication page, she passed on December 21st to be with God. We were grateful for all the plans and things we set up for the family during our 43 years and very thankful that we allowed God to work in our lives. I pray that you will do the same thing and raise your family according to the plans God has for you. You will not be sorry.

As I said earlier, Mary and I had some rough years, but we had a great marriage. We see that in our own children and grandchildren today. By living our lives, the way we believed God wanted us to, it made a true difference for us as a couple and a family.

Chapter 9: Children Will Test Us

As I have said before, I believe that children are born with attributes that God has instilled in them. They also have the ability to test you as their parents. They will try you almost from birth to becoming an adult. How you as a parent handle these tests will greatly determine how the kids will turn out.

Children, as well as adults, need love, acceptance and discipline. It is very important for children to receive these attributes especially the discipline. They need these attributes in their lives, so they can grow up and become good citizens, as well as have a well-rounded life. All three of the attributes, love, acceptance and discipline are important and they all need to be consistent. There are going to be times when your children test you that your love and acceptance of them may falter, but as long as the discipline is consistent, the children will trust and love you. The purpose of testing you is to find out what they can and cannot get away with.

Children know what they need as we discussed in another chapter and part of that need is to have mom and dad discipline them when they do wrong. Children will do things wrong just to test you and find out what you will do about it. Maybe you have noticed or even did yourself as a child that when sent to your room, you ranted and raved, but in your heart you were saying thank you to your parents. You do not have to admit to that if you do not want to.

It is very important that a child is given the same discipline each time they do something they are not supposed to do. In other words, set a particular discipline for each different thing that your child does wrong. Keeping it the same will give your child security that they will know and appreciate. This will also show them that you love them and accept them for who they really are. One of the popular ways to discipline is the one, two, three method. If the child does not respond to the counting method, then a consistent punishment should be given. If you have to repeat this method, then be consistent. The child will soon grow to believe and appreciate that particular method. If you are not consistent, the child will see that they are getting away with it and will keep trying until you stick to your guns. It is also important to have set rules for the children to follow and for you as the parents to follow those rules in your disciplining of your children. You as their parents need to develop the discipline that you will use and the method that you believe will work the best for your family. Consistency is vital in all areas of raising children.

Do children want to do and be bad? In my years of experience, I have found that not to be true. If the parents let the children get away with doing bad things, it will affect the child's self-esteem in a negative manner. It could also affect them for the rest of their life, if they are not disciplined in the home. If you let your children get away without disciplining them, you are in fact telling them that you don't love them like you should and you also don't accept them for who they really are. Children, like you were when you were their age, will do almost anything they can to test the parents. If you have more than one child in the home, they will fight amongst themselves for attention. When they test you, they are trying to find out where they fit in the family as well as society.

Testing by children should not be taken as a mark against you as parents, but as a challenge to you to take each situation, evaluate it, and then act on it. It may take, which I recommend, physical touching rather than yelling or getting mad. When your child tests you and you handle it with love, you will get a better response from the child, than if you yell at them or get mad at them. True love can cover a multitude of sins and prevent a lot of bad things from happening. When a child tests you, and they win, believe it or not they are disappointed. The tests that they give you are designed for them to lose. In other words, if they lose the test, they win the game. By that I mean, the game of life. This shows them that you truly love them and care about them enough to not let them get away with things they should not and do not want to get away with. We must remember that God created your child in His image. That should be self-explanatory for those who believe in God. If you spend the time needed by your children, you will be able to see if they are testing you or not. When they test, they show signs of what they are up to, that you as a parent will learn to notice after watching them over a period.

Another thing about the testing that children will use is, like we have said before, that children will do as you do, not necessarily what you say. This gives the child the advantage, because they are watching you and seeing how you react to different situations. This gives them the advantage when they want to test. This should be a clue to you to also watch how you are acting around your children. They pick up more than most people realize. It is also very important that you check on what your children are doing. If they tell you that something they were asked to do is finished, you need to check on them. This is a test that all kids will perform and that is to not do what you say and see if they can get away with it. After a period of time, you can develop more of a trust for your child and when they say they have done what they were asked to do, you won't have to question it, but just believe them. This will give them the encouragement they need to know they are doing the right thing and can be trusted.

During the testing period, that lasts most of their years at home, they will change testing methods as you find each one out, and try something else. It is part of the testing game. When they realize that you will not let them get away with things, they will slow the testing down and make changes as needed. Do not be fooled when they start doing everything that you want them to do. They are just working on new tests to perform on you.

Testing by children is good. It, to some degree, makes it a game between parents and children to help them to be more acquainted with each other and gain respect and trust for each other. This will also give the child a more secure station not only in the home but also in life itself.

The testing of parents by the children is vitally important and if parents fail to respond positively they will be letting them down. We all need boundaries in our lives especially children. I know what happened to me when boundaries were not set for me as a child. I deliberately did things that were wrong to get my parents to help me through the struggles and show me that they cared. It didn't work for me, but you as a parent have an opportunity to help your children by paying attention and listening to what they have to say.

What I am saying is that you really need to be aware of the testing your children are doing and make sure you handle them properly. You will not be sorry. If you win the tests, the children will be a lot happier.

I would like to challenge you as parents to find ways to recognize the tests that your children use on you. It would also be a good idea to come up with consistent dealings with each test and not change them from one time to the next. They will test you the same way until they know they cannot get away with it. Believe me; once they know they can't get away with a test, they will be very happy with you as their parents. Your children expect you to love, accept and discipline them.

Chapter 10: When a Child Is Abused

Abuse of a child in any fashion is inexcusable in any situation. No child deserves to be abused, no matter what they do or how they act. It is unforgivable to harm a child in any way. Children cannot defend themselves against abuse for the most part since they are usually weaker than their abuser. One might ask, why is this subject part of a parenting book. The answer to that question is that in today's society, most children are abused by parents or someone in the family. That is a sad statement to make and to hear, but it is true. That is why I am addressing the issue in this parenting book. I believe that anyone who is an abuser, by having a true belief in God, can turn their life around Every child is a very precious gift from God and deserves only the best of love and care.

What is abuse? Three abuses that can have an effect on children are physical, sexual and emotional abuses. It is my belief that the emotional abuse is the worst of the three. I will go into each one of the abuses in detail and you can decide for yourself how to react to them. I must warn you that the detail can and will be explicit because I believe that it is important enough to let you know as much about them as possible. I do not have all the answers, but will give as much information as I can from what I know through working with people in this area. This would be a good point to bring out the importance of reporting abuse of any kind to someone who could help.

Physical Abuse:

We will begin with the physical abuse. Physical abuse is the most obvious because of the evidence left on the child being abused. Like I mentioned before, there is no excuse for hitting a child, as a form of punishment or any other reason. Spanking a child in an appropriate manner is okay because as the scripture says, "spare the rod spoil the child". Physical abuse can and does take on quite a few forms. Depending on the size and age of the child, the damage inflicted can be varied as far as how it will affect the child. Physical abuse can and has caused death to a minor child. I have dealt with three people, in the county jail, who have either lost a child by death or caused a child to die because of the physical abuse they inflicted. This type of abuse can and does cause devastating pain on survivors as well as perhaps amazing guilt on the one who caused the death. Sadly, it will ruin many lives needlessly.

When one hit's a child, several things can happen, such as bruising, perhaps breaking arms or legs, up to leaving permanent damage to the child. Shaken baby syndrome can leave a child with brain damage for the rest of their lives. Unfortunately, it is too late to stop the abuse once it has already taken place. The damage is done and those involved will have to live with it for the rest of their lives. There are many reasons that can cause physical abuse to occur. One of the main reasons for physical abuse of a child is the economy. That is not a legitimate excuse, but when parents are struggling, perhaps their tempers are a little easier to set off when they are trying to make ends meet or trying to handle other problems in the home. Taking care of a child is difficult enough when things are going right, but when outside influences interfere, it makes it seem impossible. This is one of the reasons that parents to be need to learn as much as possible about raising a child prior to giving birth. Physical abuse, even in the hardest times, can be prevented if the parents use the right methods to avoid it.

I believe that when parents see that they are going to have a major disagreement on an issue, they can avoid getting the child involved by taking prior planned steps to make sure the child is not in the middle of the disagreement. If a child is starting to do something to irritate mom or dad, it is best for the other parent to take care of the child until they can resolve their differences. All differences can be worked out if everybody agrees that they want to work them out. I do not want to confuse spanking a child as being physical abuse because a swat on the behind of a small child can and has been good discipline. Of course, spanking can get out of control and should only be used when deemed necessary by a parent.

As we talked about early on in the book, all people need discipline, especially children. Each parent must learn how to discipline in the correct way, not only for the child, but also for you. When one takes discipline to far, it can become physical abuse. I really believe that few parents actually want to harm their child unless they themselves have altered their mood with drugs, alcohol or some other method, especially if they wanted the child.

Physical abuse can scar a child for life. God did not create the body to be abused and abusing it whether by our own means or by abusing another human being such as a child is truly against what God had in mind for His children. The smaller a child is, the easier it is to do permanent damage to their body when they are physically abused. You can break bones; do irreversible brain and physical damage that could scar the child for the rest of their life. Once physical abuse or any other abuse occurs, it is too late to reverse the problems that can or may occur because of the abuse.

Another side affect of physical abuse is that your child may grow up to be a physical abuser himself. After all, since he grew up with it, it could be natural for him to think it is right and inflict pain on others. If you recall my story, I was abused physically and I in turn did harm to others before I realized that it was not the right thing to do. What we learn as a child, for the most part, will be carried on into our adulthood. It can be changed if we make the decision to change our life style to one of more value. For me, that was the acceptance of God, as my Lord and Savior. It really does work.

Unless a parent is totally off the deep end, they will most always regret the physical abuse they inflict on their child. Unfortunately, it comes after the abuse has been applied. When you raise a hand or an object up to a child, you intend to do harm to that child. That is why if you or your spouse feel that things might get to that point, it is a great idea to have the spouse who is still in control remove the child from the scene. This will give both of the parents the opportunity to cool down and gather their thoughts, discuss what was about to take place and make the changes that are necessary to perhaps avoid this situation from coming up again. By taking precautions and using pre-learning that we talked about early on in the book, you can avoid so many of these problems and live a happier life with your family. I believe that talking to God through prayer at a time like this will offer you the best advice that you can get. It would also be a good idea to sit down with your child and talk about what almost happened and apologize for what you were about to do.

The pain that a child will have to endure other, than the physical pain, will be the feeling of not being loved and accepted by his parents. This is usually when children will fall prey to drugs, alcohol and other undesirable things the world has to offer. At this point, you can only hope and pray, that your child will find the Lord, if he has not already. The bottom line with physical abuse is that it is harmful to everyone involved. The person receiving the abuse will suffer physical pain and the one who gives the abuse will suffer self-imposed mental abuse. Neither one will be of much value. There is so much violence in television and music that it can catch your children off guard and even give them ideas that they do not need to have about imposing physical abuse on others, especially those people your child does not get along with. This is a very good reason to teach your children proper values as they are growing up. It would be a good idea to monitor what they watch on television and what music they listen too. It wouldn't hurt to monitor their friends and also keep up with what they are doing on the internet. There is a lot of problems on the internet that children should avoid.

Sexual Abuse:

The next abuse we will discuss is sexual abuse. Sexual abuse is growing in our society at a rapid pace. Someone who was sexually abused themselves or has the wrong values of human behavior that were taught when they were growing up usually performs sexual abuse on another person because they believe that is the right thing to do. Physical abuse is easier to overcome than sexual abuse. Sexual abuse, especially on a child, takes their innocence away from them. They experience things that they should never have to. Sexual abuse occurs when someone touches another person inappropriately, or even worse makes them do things that are not normal behavior.

Why would someone want to sexually abuse someone? Especially a child, you might ask. That is a good question. I will try to elaborate on that question by sharing some examples and some reasons. First, it is my personal belief that it usually starts in the home of the abused. The parents may have been abused themselves whether sexually or some other way when they were growing up. In cases like this, the abused can and will carry that on in their own lives. I know because it happened to me. To my knowledge God is the only one who can take the desire away from a person. When a child is abused at home or abused by a friend, neighbor or someone else, it can show them that is the way to show love to someone. It can also anger the abused to the point that they want to hurt someone else by abusing them. Can an abuser be changed? Of course, they can. I was an abuser, which I shared in another chapter. It was not until I accepted Jesus Christ as my Lord and Savior that I stopped being an abuser. The world says that once an abuser, always an abuser. Believe me that is not true. Like with any other bad habit or vice, Jesus can change a person's behavior, if they let Him. Some of what we see on television, movies or the music we listen to also has an affect on how a person acts. It is very important that we monitor not only what our children, but also what we as parents watch or listen too. As we have said before, parents are the most influential people in a child's life.

What effects can sexual abuse, especially to a child, have? I would say that the most damaging could be the loss of trust in people. If someone they trust abuses them, they will lose that trust, not only for the abuser, but for other people in their life. Trust is, in my opinion, the most important attribute in a person's life. If they cannot be trusted, they will have lost a feeling that may be permanent. There is also the problem of having a fear of people, not knowing whether they will harm them or not. Will the abused ever be able to put it behind them and move on with their lives? Of course. I certainly did. For me it took a relationship with God and He allowed me to move on with my life. This is where forgiving and not necessarily forgetting comes into play. We need to forgive the abuser, and try to forget what happened to us. I have always believed that it doesn't hurt to reflect on the past to see how far we have come but we shouldn't let anything that happened before cause us to do something that we shouldn't.

Why does sexual abuse happen, especially to a child? The biggest reason is the abuse that happened to one during their childhood. Like with me, I became an abuser after being abused when I was five years old. They say that once an abuser always an abuser. That is not always true. I was an abuser after being abused and with the help of God, even though it was still a part of me, I was able to overcome being an abuser. I still believe that the feelings are still in my heart, but because of God I don't act on the feelings. I believe that God is the only person who can truly help any abuser whether it is a physical, sexual or emotional abuser. There are other reasons of course, but the main reason is because of it happening to a child while he is growing up. God has given all people, including children, the ability to know right from wrong. They need to be taught what is right and what is wrong as far as the actual event but there are some that people, especially children, know is wrong. One of those is good touch, bad touch. I believe God protects His children by supplying that information prior to their birth.

Emotional abuse:

We have talked about physical and sexual abuse and the problems they cause for their victims. Now let us talk about what I believe to be the worst of the three abuses and that is emotional abuse. Why would I believe that emotional abuse is the worst? I will explain my reasoning after we have discussed the emotional abuse. You may not and certainly do not have to agree with my reasons, but as we have said before, everyone must make their own decisions in this life. Now on to the problems and reasons that emotional abuse occurs. Emotional abuse can and does occur to people of all ages. This abuse can seriously harm a person's self-esteem as well as how they treat others. If you tell a boy that "he's a good boy" one hundred times and tell him one time that "he is a bad boy". Which one do you think will affect him the most? Believe it or not, he will remember the one that "he is a bad boy" over "he is a good boy". You can imagine what that will do to his self-esteem. I do not have the answer as to why he will remember the bad one over the good one, but I have seen it work and that is what affected me the most. That is the reason that I did the things I did as a child. I did not care a whole lot about myself. In other words, I had low self-esteem.

Emotional abuse can and does scar a person for life unless major changes can occur in their life. It is important, especially to children, to be built up not torn down. They will pattern their life after the way they are treated at home. Even though they are treated badly when they are out in the world, they will respond to the way they are treated at home, more than to their friends and other people they will run into outside of the home. As I have said before, I was abused physically, sexually and emotionally. I also passed this on to victims of my own, until I realized that was not the life I really wanted. There were people in my life that also wanted the best for me and they helped me to find God. Once I started living my life for God, things started getting better, I gave those horrible abuses to Him, and He helped me to be where I am today. He continues to help me every day.

The reason I say that emotional abuse is the worst of the three abuses is as follows. Emotional abuse attacks the self-esteem of an individual. It can and does make a person think less of themselves than they truly deserve. The more a person is abused emotionally, the lower the self-esteem gets and the less a person will feel good about themselves. It can make a person feel worthless and cause them to do and say things that they may not normally do or say. These things can be harmful not only to themselves but to others because when a person's self-esteem is low enough, they will do things that they would normally not do such as hurting someone or themselves just to name a few.

Recap of abuse:

I want to recap about the abuse of a child. There is absolutely no reason that a child should be abused in any way. A child is defenseless against an adult. Any adult that harms a child in any way should be punished to the full extent of the law. How and what can an adult do to prevent any of the three abuses from happening? First, I believe an adult who cannot control their anger should not be around children. Children need and want to be loved, accepted and disciplined not harmed, whether physically, emotionally or sexually.

When a child is born, they are born into this world to bring joy to not only their family, but to all those they are around. After all, this child is a gift of God and has an express purpose on this earth. God does have a plan for all people and it is up to us to find out what that plan is and then act upon it. How do we know what that plan is? If we read the Bible and pray to God, He will give us the directions that we need, to complete that plan. One thing for sure, and that is, He does not want anyone, let alone His children, to be abused in any way. God has given us warnings about not harming a hair on one of His children's head.

How do we handle this problem of abuse of a child? First, I believe people, especially parents, should educate themselves in the proper care of a child. This book has been written to address that issue, as well as many others, about being a parent who will love and raise their children in the proper manner. We talked in earlier chapters about the importance of choosing the right lifestyle and selecting the right mate. If this is done properly, the chances of you harming your child will be almost nil. If you, as parents, have the right ideals set up in your life, even when you experience problems such as financial, health or others, you will be able to go on living your lives as God has taught you without taking it out on your children.

It is my prayer that you and your spouse live a life filled with joy and happiness and that your children will prosper as you have. I just ask that you keep God at the center of your lives. Remember, this book is based on one man's personal life's experience of sixty years and hopefully will give you good information to help you in your family life. The most important book that you can read and follow, in my opinion, is the Bible.

There is no excuse for abusing people, especially children. Children are a true gift from God and need to receive the respect that they truly deserve. No matter how bad a child acts, they do not deserve to be abused.

I would like to challenge you to find ways that you can prevent any kind of abuse in your home as well as other places. All people need to be loved not hurt.

Chapter 11: The Importance of Grandparents

In years past, grandparents were very instrumental, in helping raise their grandchildren. That practice seems to have gone to the wayside over the years. It is a practice that shouldn't be ignored in this author's opinion. So what are some of the benefits of grandparents helping raise their grandchildren? The first and I believe foremost is that they have a stake in not only their grandchildren but also their own children. Most grandparents want to see their families succeed and that is a great thing.

We often lose the love and information that grandparents can pass on to their grandchildren. Many times, there may be a problem between grandparents and their children or they do not necessarily want the help they have and can offer.

I was one who did not have the advantage of grandparents because my parents did not necessarily want me around them or my grandparents. I believe that I missed many opportunities by not having them in my life.

One of the main reasons that I say that grandparents are very important in a families life is that we have noticed that there is a change in our society that people have become more interested in what they want and not necessarily what is best for the family. It is my belief that our generation needs to make changes as far as how we treat our grandparents. Grandparents lived during a different time of life and experienced things that can be extremely helpful to your family. Times change, people change and the economy changes as the years go by and we have a choice as how that will affect our family. There are times that grandparents may have answers to the problems you are going through because they have lived through them.

Grandparents can and will make good babysitters, companions and excellent teachers for their grandchildren. As a grandfather myself, I love spending time with my grandkids because we have fun. We also have some serious times that we do important things. Mary would have the grandkids over one or two days a week. They would help us plant the garden and even help clean up their messes in the house. One of the things that most grandkids like to do is help grandparents in the kitchen. This is valuable training for the grandkids because it not only teaches them to do positive things but is a big help to grandparents. Spending time together with grandparents, parents and the grand children has a positive effect on all concerned and can only be healthy for all if all participate in a positive manner. It gives three generations of a family the opportunity to share with one another and to enjoy each other's company. Grandparents can have a lasting effect on their grandchildren by sharing with them life's stories and how they handled things when they were young and growing up. I believe children are very interested in the history of their family and not only need, but want to find out as much as they can. This information will help them as they are growing up. Grandparents can give the children valuable instruction that will also help as they grow. Like I have said before, experience is the best teacher in almost every aspect of our lives. Grandparents have experiences that when shared with the grandchildren, can truly make a difference in their lives. They can avoid some pitfalls that they might otherwise fall into. You might think that you as their parents should be able to share and you can, but grandparents can share from their generation and experience. Having both parents and grandparents sharing gives the children two different views to help them make up their own minds.

We need to understand, three generations of the family working together can be a problem, if not all agree on how to do it. The parents have the primary responsibility to raise and teach their children and to let the grandparents know when they can step into the situation. It is also very helpful if the parents and grandparents meet to set up boundaries for how each fits into the picture. The one thing that needs to be avoided, is arguing about who does what in front of the children. They need positive input not negative.

Grandparents have the privilege of spoiling the grandchildren and it really is not a bad thing in my opinion. It helps them to form a bond with each other and that is very special. That can also get out of hand, so it needs to be kept at a minimum. Grandparents definitely should not override the rules set down by the parents. This would only cause confusion for the children and problems with the parents. Bottom line is that if both parents and grandparents are coordinated, you can avoid many problems. By avoiding problems, you can create a valuable tool for raising children to be the best they can possibly be. Does this mean there will be no problems? Of course not, but it will certainly keep them to a minimum. There will always be problems in a home, but it is up to the parents to solve them whether it involves mom, dad, the children or all.

I have witnessed, throughout my life, several situations where grandparents were involved and most, if treated right, worked out very well. It definitely takes each person in the family playing their part and not trying to tell others what or how to do things. That means that everybody has a place in the family and if all agree, it will be a blessing to all involved.

We must realize that we are all human beings made in the image of God, but because we are human and make mistakes, not everything will be perfect. We must accept the fact that there will be disagreements in all families and it is up to the people in that family to make it work with God's help.

Grandparents are important in all families. If they are included, they can offer good quality information and examples for everyone in the family.

They can give help by sharing some of their experiences growing up and give a different outlook for the whole family.

I would like to challenge you to think of some ways that your parents can be helpful to your children. As we said earlier, grandparents can offer many ways to help not only you but your children as well.

CHAPTER 12: HELPFUL HINTS

I want to spend some time talking about some of the things that may come up while raising your children. They may seem like common sense things and some of them are, but several things we seem to take for granted. These are issues that I would like to talk about and perhaps even give some helpful hints about. I will be sharing from personal experiences that I have lived through when raising my own children. I have also learned how ignoring these simple suggestions can have an adverse effect on children as well as the whole family. I would like to believe that all parents want the best for their family, especially their children. Unfortunately, due to economic times and society in general, it makes things difficult for families that need the help. It is my hope and prayer that the information in this book will indeed make a difference in how you and your family prosper in this world. Now that we have made the introduction, let us get down to the real business of raising children.

There are several things that I would like to share with you and hopefully they will be a help to you in raising your children. They will be in random order because every family will be different and will be able to take these helpful hints and arrange them in an order that will best fit their needs. So let us begin the list of helpful hints and see where they take us.

Setting Goals and plans:

The first one that I would like to discuss is setting up goals and plans prior to children becoming a part of your family. These can be simple plans such as who will take care of the responsibilities for the children when they come into the home. If both parents work outside of the home then they will have to spend more time working out the details of who is going to do what when they return home from work. If you can help each other and be willing to fill in for each other, you will find the work of raising your child will become more fun. By no means do I want to say that you will not have challenges because those are automatic in every relationship whether with children or not. However, getting back to setting goals and plans, it does not hurt to have measures set up for baby-sitting, like with grandparents or friends.

This gives you the opportunity in a tough time to get away and regroup with each other. Believe it or not, parents who do not have plans set up can get into trouble with saying or doing something to the child or each other that you may regret. I do not want to alarm you, but prevention of a problem is easier than having to do intervention after the fact. I believe that most parents who abuse their children in any way, do not want to, but are pushed into it because of not having the right upbringing themselves or not having help available to them from family or friends. This is one of the reasons grandparents are so important in a family. I have seen it work both ways and the parents that get things in place before the children arrive have a much better time adapting to each other. It even makes their lives much better and enjoyable.

Paying attention to your children:

Another helpful hint is, once you have children, that you pay attention to each child and develop goals for each one. For the most part, each one will be unique and will have different goals which is not a bad thing since we are all individuals and have individual needs and desires. Now do not get me wrong, I am not referring to goals for their lives when they grow up and decide what they want to do in life. I am referring to goals that will help them to grow and mature as fine young adults. As they grow, you can help them by sitting down and discussing what they want and you can help them to develop that goal or through discussion make goals that will meet all of your families needs. This will make the child feel they are truly a part of the family and that what they have to say is important. What a self-esteem builder. Make sure to listen to your children. They can teach you as a parent, things that maybe you haven't even thought about. That is extremely important.

Setting rules for the children:

Another helpful hint is, to set up rules for the children to follow as they grow up. These rules can and should be changed for each child as they grow. Different ages require different rules. This, if the rules are followed and the children know that if they break them they will be punished, is another great self-esteem builder. When setting rules for children, it is vitally important that parents follow through. If they do not, the children will not get one of the three main things they need and that is discipline. As we have said a few times, children need love, acceptance and discipline. They will thrive on it and truly appreciate it. If they do not get this discipline, they will get the impression that mom and dad do not care. This is a real bummer on their self-esteem and can lead them to find that care from someone else. That could, and most times is, a bad thing not only for the child but also for you as parents.

I shared about setting up rules for your children and making sure that they follow them so they can grow up to appreciate rules. I think this would be a good time to tell you about Romans Chapter 13 (NIV). By reading the chapter, you will find that it shares with us that God has set into motion all authority in heaven and on the earth. This means that the laws of the land are under God's direction and need to be followed. It does not take much to see that the laws governing drivers are not being obeyed very well today. It is vitally important that you show your children that you can obey the rules. This will give them more of an incentive to follow your rules that have been set for them. Remember, children will do what you do, not necessarily what you say. If you stop for a red light or a stop sign or obey all of the other traffic laws, then your children will have your example to follow. Remember, as I have said many times, your children will do as you do not necessarily what you say.

Dealing with discipline:

I want to add another helpful hint that also deals with discipline and that is, do not threaten your children with discipline and not carry through. By that I mean don't tell them your going to do something, such as cut off their allowance, spank them or send them to their rooms if they do not comply with your request unless you follow through. You want your children to follow the rules that you have all agreed on because they want to and ideally, it needs to be done that way. Occasionally the children will test you on the direction you give them, but this is where you must stay strong and stick to the rules set up rather than make idle threats. The children will appreciate it in the end.

Discipline is an extremely positive helpful hint. Without discipline, you tell your children as well as yourself, that you do not care about them or your spouse. Without discipline, you have a home that will be chaotic at best. Children will test you as parents as often and in as many ways as possible to find out what they can get away with and how you as parents will react. Therefore, it is your responsibility as parents, to make sure you stay in tune with your children so you discipline them as needed. They will also, as we have said before, need love and acceptance. It will also show them that you can be trusted because you keep your word. If you discipline them, they will know you love and accept them for who they are. A very important attribute, don't you think?

Develop a summer activity calendar:

A very positive helpful hint is to develop a summer activity calendar with the whole family. It is very important to get the children involved with this activity so they can have a part in picking out activities that they would like to be involved in. I have seen it work in my family quite successfully. I cannot think of one thing that is negative about this calendar. It is a tool that can bring the family together at the dinner table or any other place you choose. It gives each member of the family the opportunity to give input as to what activities they would like to do. It will make quite an impact on the children, because they will have a chance to have their voice heard, and have their ideas acted upon. This will help the children to feel that they are truly part of the family. Once the calendar is finished, display it where everybody can see it. That way everybody will know what they will be doing everyday during the summer. Of course there will be changes as family responsibilities change, but you can discuss these options at the planning session. Anything that you as parents can do to involve the children is a good positive thing. This can and will be a positive self-esteem builder, and you know how important that is, for everybody. After all, children are an important part of the family.

Setting up final papers:

Another helpful hint that I believe to be very important and that is to set up final papers and have them readily available in case they are needed. We found that to be a very important process to have done prior to Mary's passing. You may wonder, what does this have to do with parenting? Well as I said earlier, anything that can be done to help the family, including the children, is a good thing. It can teach them responsibility so they can take care of these things when they become parents. Remember, children will do what their parents do, not necessarily what they say. This can be a fantastic teaching tool and can help your children to respect and trust you more. They can see that you are taking responsibility for the family and they will learn how they can do the same thing when the time comes. I would hope that you would have family meetings to work on these, as well as other important issues, that will further help teach that responsibility to your children.

I have, as perhaps you have, seen or heard about people who did not have things in order when a death occurred in the family. It can be devastating to the survivors and can actually tear the family apart. I have experienced that in my own family. Mary and I both decided that we did not want to put that burden on our family. I want to share here that it was vitally important to my whole family when Mary passed that we had all the necessary papers already filled out. I have all of my things sitting in a cabinet and my children both have a key so all they have to do, when the time comes, open it and all the papers will be there to take care of my arrangements and financial obligations. It made a difference in my home and I am sure it will do the same for you. Obviously, we do not want to use the papers, but we all know that the time will come for all of us. I believe that anything we can do to help the family should be done. Sometimes life deals us a bad hand, so if there is anything that we can do to make things better, we should.

Family meetings:

Another helpful hint that we have touched on, that I would like to go more in depth about, is family meetings. Family meetings are very important in a family. It gives each member the opportunity to speak their mind and offer suggestions as to how things can be done to help the family. Like the summer activity calendar, the meetings should be set on the calendar so each person knows when they are. That way everybody can set their schedules to be able to make the meetings. Of course, the younger children will need more help preparing than the older children and you as the parents. These meetings can and will be a learning tool for the children to teach them more responsibility. These family meetings can be quite useful if everybody is truly honest about things that are talked about. These meetings can help the children to get true answers about things that they are seeing and hearing in school or wherever they hang out. If your child comes home and tells you that he was offered drugs but he turned them down you should compliment him. It is great that you have a good enough relationship, that he would come home and talk to you about it.

That is a major step right there. How you respond to them, will make a difference in the results that will occur. You have two choices and that is to blow up and yell at him or sit and share with him that he made the best choice. I truly believe that your children will really appreciate how you are handling things and their trust and respect for you will grow. Everything you do that is positive, will affect the children and they will grow to love you more, because you are doing the right things with them. They have many wants but they also have many needs, which are more important to them, truth be told. Dad has a very important role in the family and that is to lead the family closer to Christ every day. He needs to set the example and follow the teachings of the scriptures. There are two basic elements of family worship and they are reading the Bible and praying. I would suggest starting these worship meetings with prayer and invite God into your meeting. I would also suggest these worship meetings can be the close of the regular family meeting and after dismissal; each person can go ahead and do the things they need to.

Chores and responsibilities:

Another helpful hint that we may have touched on a little, but I want to expand on, is giving children chores and responsibilities. These will change as a child grows but it will teach them the importance of doing things around the house as well as in the outside world. Children need to learn as early as possible how to take responsibility for their actions whether bad or good. This will teach them that there are consequences for every action. They will learn that when they do the right thing, they will receive a positive reaction as opposed to a negative reaction for doing the wrong thing. This is extremely good for a child, because this will enhance their self-esteem and help them to gain trust and respect for you as their parents. Believe me, that trust and respect has to be earned by the whole family. It is not a free gift. You cannot assume that you can trust or respect anyone. They need to show you that they can be trusted and respected. Another important thing that will develop from children having chores and responsibilities is they will take pride in themselves, which is a great builder of self-esteem. Like we have said before, self-esteem is the measure of a persons self worth. In other words, it shows what they think of and how they feel about themselves.

Getting upset at times:

This is a short but sweet helpful hint. All parents will get upset at times. All people have a natural reaction. It can occur over a variety of different things such as losing a game, having an accident, getting upset with someone in the family and many more. Some of the ways to overcome results of getting upset is to walk it off, go off by yourself yelling, talking it out with someone or if it gets to bad, you can hit something. What I am sharing with you is, if you start to get upset with your spouse or your children, you need to get completely away from the situation and cool down. If you do not, you may find yourself doing something that you may regret for the rest of your life. By that I mean you may do harm to your family that cannot be repaired. So bottom line, make sure you learn and practice walking away when you get upset or angry. You will not regret it. It will give you the opportunity to think about the problem and how you can handle it the next time it happens. It will also help you to get a better handle on your own emotions and how you can change them. I would encourage you to consult God during this time in addition to all other times because He is the only one who can truly help you, if you let Him.

Children's friends

I have another helpful hint, and that is as follows. Children all need friends in addition to their family. That is quite natural because they go to school with friends, have friends in the neighborhood and occasionally meet new friends when they go places. It is very difficult to be a parent and a friend. A parent needs to be there to raise their children, have fun with them and trust them. A friend is one they can also have fun with and even grow to trust. They may be able to share things with friends that they may not be able to share with you as their parents. Now to the helpful hint. I have experienced several times over the years, that when kids stay overnight or just spend time with friends, they may not have the proper supervision. This can and does lead to some things happening that are not good. It is my personal belief, from experience and from seeing it happen in many homes, that it is vitally important for you as their parents to know your children's friends parents before letting them spend time at their friends home. Your children may fight this idea as an invasion of their privacy, but they will truly appreciate it in the end because they will know that you really care about them and what they are doing outside of the home.

This will enforce the trust and love that you have for your children. They will truly appreciate it even though they may not show it. When kids are with other kids, it is easier to go along with the crowd then to stick up for what they believe. That is commonly called . . . peer pressure.

It would be a good idea to meet your children's friends and talk to their parents before they start hanging out at their friend's house or even at your house. This will help everybody to be more comfortable with each other especially the children. Be open to letting your kids have their friends over to visit and even stay overnight. If you keep order and are raising your kid's right, you will see that your kids will have a great time and love you for it. A happy home is one where all kids will be comfortable and they will want to have their friends over. Mary and I followed these rules and our children and their friends had no problems with the rules, and we all got along great. Of course, things weren't perfect, but definitely a lot better than if we didn't know their friends and their parents.

Technology:

I would like to talk about one more helpful hint and that is technology. Technology is a great thing and over the many years has been a great help to our world. Technology in the medical and the law professions are two that I can think of right off hand that have made marvelous strides to help take care of people and make sure people who commit crimes are treated professionally and have their rights protected as well as protecting the citizens. Some of the new trends today are cell phones, ipods, computers and of course the internet.

I believe that all of these things are good. It is the abuse of these things that are causing the problems. Everything on God's green earth is good since He has created all things or has given people the ability to create and invent things. It is people who use what has been created that can cause the problem. As far as children having these things, that is up to the parents to make that decision. I believe that the children need to be taught the proper use of technology the same as anything else they deal with. It is widely known that use of the cell phone for not only talking but for texting, is causing problems. Children who are not taught correctly may use them for cheating in school, or communicating with people they should not. In addition, the cell phone is causing problems in all parts of our society.

Another problem that is becoming popular among young people is sexting. They send sexually explicit pictures to friends who may pass them on. These pictures can and sometimes do find there way to the internet. Not only is it wrong, but it is or can be illegal. It is up to parents to teach their children the proper way to use the phone so they will not cause problems or get into trouble. Parents also need to monitor the time that the cell phones are being used. Are the children abusing the phones? If they are not monitored or do not have rules as to when they can use the cell phone, then the parent doesn't really know where their children are, what they are doing or who they are with. While on the subject of technology, I believe from what I have seen and heard that parents need to pay more attention to their children's use of the internet.

The internet can be used for good of course, but there are people who are using the internet to find ways to harm children and take advantage of them. There are things such as porno out on the internet that nobody should have to see especially children. There are many dangers on the internet and because you don't necessarily know where they are from, it is dangerous to get into some of these sites. Another thing that I believe is a problem with the internet and that is that children are using it to get book reports and other information for school that doesn't require them to do much learning or thinking for themselves. I would make the following suggestion, but you will have to make the decision yourself. I would not suggest letting kids have computers in their rooms unless you can monitor what they are doing on the internet and of course the computer itself. If you raise your children correctly and that is according to what God has planned for you, you will have a much better chance of trusting them with the computers and anything else they may have.

It is important that parents monitor the amount of time that a child spends on the internet and what they are involved with. I personally think it is a big mistake to let children have a computer in their room, especially with the door closed. I believe it needs to be in a place where all can access it and it can be easily seen by parents. It is a decision that you as the parents must make. Remember, you are responsible to God for how you raise your children. I also believe that instead of listening to what the producers of movies, television programs and music are rating them as, you as a parent should check them out for yourselves and make sure they would be ok for your children to see or listen to. May you make the right choice.

Sexual relations and our kids:

There is one more yet very important helpful hint that I would like to share with you and that is about sexual relations and our kids. This is a difficult situation to talk about, but it is vital due to the ever-increasing interest in sexual relations amongst our kids today. We are a curious people and it is normal for kids to be inquisitive about many things that they are around daily. They see sex on television and movies, hear about it in the music they listen to and hear about it at school and other places that they may be. Sex is a big subject that kids talk about with their friends. As a child grows up their body begins to change and there are feelings that they are not familiar with and obviously want to find out what they are and how they affect them. I believe girls are more prone to this because they go through more changes than a boy does.

I have had a couple of situations in my life that proved to me that when kids start going through puberty, they need even more help then normal. I had two experiences with two different girls that were each 13 when it happened. The first was a girl that I knew and helped take care of for several years because her mom was divorced and she did not have a father at home. I had become the father in that home and spent time with her and her twin brother filling in the father role. One day I was sitting in the kitchen and mom was outside in the yard when the girl came into the house and raised her sweater up to reveal her developing breasts. The most important reaction to that incident was that it was never brought up again. The second girl, that I was not as close to, asked me to go with her to get her first bras. Her situation was the same in that she did not have a father that cared much for her. This was a situation that the girl wanted to show her dad that she was growing up. Both of these situations were completely normal and proved to me that boys and girls need their parents at different times in their lives to help them through difficult situations.

If mom and dad are not there and there is not a replacement role model, the children will find what they need elsewhere. This is where our children find themselves getting into major problems. Remember, it is normal for children to have these feelings and I believe that it is perfectly ok as long as it is handled correctly. I am sure you had them when you were growing up. I urge you mom and dad to take special care to watch for the signs from your children, not only about sex but also every sign that they will give. They will give these signs off and will need your help. The Bible is clear on sexual behavior for everyone so you might want to read up on it, pray about it and let God help you through it. The most important aspect of these situations is that both girls were happy and it showed them that I cared about them. It also helped to keep them out of trouble.

Moms, if your son wants you to do or talk about things, make a point of being open to it no matter what the subject. It is for both of your benefits. It may very well keep him out of trouble later and you from heartbreak. Dads, you have the same responsibility as mom only with your daughter. It may be awkward at first, but believe me, you will not be disappointed nor will your children. In fact, they will truly appreciate what you are doing for them even if it does not appear that they do. The bottom line is this. Parents need to be responsible for all aspects of their children's lives. Honesty is the absolute best possible way to raise your children. There should be no subject that you can't talk to them about and answer their questions about. Remember, if you don't take care of them, I guarantee that they will find someone who will. I don't believe you would really want that. When your children want to talk about sex, make sure you are honest and answer their questions to the best of your ability. I strongly recommend that both parents be ready to talk to their children about anything that they want to talk about.

Finances:

One other important issue to deal with is finances. With things changing so quickly in our society, it would be a good idea to take time to work on what is important in your family. Make a budget and stick with it. It is always a good idea to put money away in savings, 401K or other ways that can help insure that when you retire or if you lose your job or anything else that may happen in our society today that you and your family will be able to stay on target with your lives.

Recap of helpful hints:

We talk about all of these helpful hints to give you some ideas that may work for you and your family. You need to feel free to use as many or as few of them according to the needs you have in your individual family. Not all hints will work for all families but I do know they do work. Try them and with God's help see what a difference it can make in your home.

As the children grow, you will find these helpful hints; although they may change now and then will be very helpful in raising your children. The children will have different needs as they grow, but the rules for all practical purposes will stay the same. These helpful hints will help keep your children from going along with their friend's ideas and thoughts. I believe all families need rules to discipline their children, but I am realistic enough to say that is not always true. It just takes looking around to see how the younger generation is doing to realize that not all homes have the discipline rules in force. The children will suffer in the end, but the parents will eventually suffer, if they care about their children at all, but it could be too late to do anything about it. Believe it or not, all our kids really need and want is to be loved, accepted and disciplined. If they get these three things while they are growing up, and you as parents are truly interested in their welfare, you will be amazed at the results when they are adults.

I would like to challenge you to take the information in this chapter and find other ways that you can make your home a better place for your whole family. I believe you will be surprised at how little it takes to make a truly happy home if you really try.

Chapter 13: Individual Roles in the Family

I believe that God has given each of us a personal role to play in His world. Every child that is born has a plan set for them by God and if we follow Him, we will find out what that plan is. I also believe that if we do not follow God's plan, we are on our own to live as we see fit. I know that I say a lot about my beliefs but, in my 60 some years, I have witnessed people that I know without doubt that God was allowed to be a part of their lives. I have also seen where people did not want God involved. I have seen God work in my own life and I will say that for me, it is the only way to go.

When a person reaches adulthood and thinks about having a family, they need to take a serious look at their lives. We talked about choosing the right lifestyle and that is vitally important so they can start their adult life and be the best person they can be. This speaks to the importance of raising children according to God's will. Children will carry what they learn early on in life, into adulthood with them. If their childhood was good, then the children will more than likely become successful in whatever they venture into. If their childhood was bad, things will not normally go well for them, unless a major change in their lifestyle takes place.

So what is the role of a parent? It is my belief that the role of a parent is to follow what God has planned for them and that is to; if they have children, raise them according to His will. I want to clear one thing up and that is, even though God has a plan for everyone, it does not mean that He will take you by the hand and lead you to the completion of that plan. What it does mean is that He expects us to follow His plan but has given us free choice of how we live our lives. If we spend time in prayer and reading the scriptures, God will show us how to work toward the plan He has for us. I can use my wife Mary's life to share why I believe this. Mary, for all practical purposes, followed what God wanted her to. The proof of that was, as I have said before, that she by all rights should have passed away 3 or 4 times prior, during her illness, to when she did. This was over an eighteen year time span. God had a purpose for her and I believe she fulfilled that purpose and was allowed to come home to be with God. Believe it or not, it made it a lot easier on the family. It was a great loss but knowing that she went to be with God was a true blessing.

Each child, like the parents, needs to have a role in the family. It does not have to be anything major, just something that they can do to help the whole family. It is not the easiest thing to assign roles to the children but it is essential for family harmony. These roles can also be talked about in the family meetings. This way each person in the family will know what is going on and this will cut down on surprises that will on occasion rise up.

The father has different roles in the family, which are as follows:
1. Provides for the basic needs of his family
2. Is generous beyond what could be expected
3. Gives his children space when they need it
4. Forgives his children…always
5. Loves his children equally, but handles each one differently.
6. Support his wife at all times.

These are in addition to his regular everyday roles.

Mom also has roles in the family that are in addition to her regular everyday roles:
1. Nurture her children
2. Discipline her children when needed
3. Love her children with all of her heart

4. Be there to nurse them back to health
5. Be a teacher to her children
6. Support her husband at all times.

Each parent has set responsibilities in the home. I believe it is God's intention that both parents work together to raise their children. (NIV Luke chapter 15) talks about the parable of the lost son. It has a powerful message. This is becoming a serious problem in our country today where children are being asked to leave or are leaving their home for various reasons. Most of the time, they are getting themselves into trouble of some kind. The parable tells us that we, as parents, should have open arms to our children when they leave for whatever reason and be ready to welcome them home. That does not mean that it will be easy, but as long as we can help our children, we must do so. Being realistic, it will not always work, but we must try the best we can to help our children. Even if we start our married life out in a positive manner and take a positive outlook on how we raise our children we can still have problems. It really is not that difficult. It just takes mom and dad putting the children in a place in their heart. We should not put anything ahead of God of course. With God being number one in our lives then comes the family.

Everyone has a role in the family. I challenge you to allow God to help you define your role and help your children define their roles to make your family life the best that it can be.

Chapter 14: What are We as Parents Doing Wrong?

We have talked all through this book about how to find and live the right lifestyle and how to choose the right mate, hopefully for life. The responsibility that we have in our family is to raise our children up in the ways that God wants us to. In this chapter, we will be dealing with why our children are having the problems they are having in our society today. It is obvious, if we look around, to see that the youth of today are suffering some severe problems. So let us take a little tour and see if we can find some ways to help or maybe even cure some of these problems. I will say that most of these problems start in the home because of parents not taking care of their responsibilities correctly.

First, the challenges that we all face, especially children, are very attractive and inviting. We look around and see people who are having fun and enjoying what this world has to offer. We also see a lot of confusion with people, not knowing for sure what to do or how to handle things. Granted the economy has a lot to do with how people act and feel. There is a lot of anger and ill feelings around us. Perhaps you have seen or even know people that demonstrate what we have just talked about. It is not pleasant to see people react as they do but each person has to take responsibility for their own actions. We will all answer to God one day for how we lived our life and it is my prayer that all will be well with you. So how do these attractions of our society affect our children?

When a family is facing financial troubles, it affects the whole family, not just the breadwinner. It causes people to say and do things they normally would not do. Usually what happens is negative. This can cause major problems in the family and to avoid things happening that someone might regret, these problems need addressing. Perhaps you remember when we talked about family meetings. It is important to talk about all aspects of the family's life at these meetings so everybody is on the same page. This should and will make a big difference in how the family handles things.

This would be a good time to talk, as a family, about either starting or rearranging the budget. Parents need to share with the kids that they are going to have to cut down on things such as going to movies and getting things they really don't need. By sharing this information with the whole family, it will give all a better feeling and appreciation for each other and the family in general.

So what are some of the problems facing our children today? Why are they facing these problems? Even more important is why are they facing these problems alone? Let us start by naming the potential problems and then talk about each one of them individually. Some of these may seem trivial, but can, if not caught early can lead to other problems. There are several, so here goes.

One is disobedience by your child. When a child disobeys mom or dad, they are testing to see what their parents will do. If you do not respond properly, you are telling your child that you do not care what they do and that you really do not love them. This is also where discipline comes into play. When a child disobeys a rule or talks back to you when you ask them to do something, that is a test to see if you mean what you say. If you discipline them, they will know you care. Remember, kids will do what you do, not necessarily what you say. Since you are showing them the correct way, they will listen and learn. Once again, be consistent in disciplining your children. You will not be sorry.

I believe a very important one is friends because children can get into a lot of trouble with their friends if we do not monitor them. We need to know who our kids are hanging out with and what they are doing. Kids do need their privacy and their fun, but they also need to obey the rules.

I believe kids need to earn their privacy by obeying the rules. You must make it a practice to know their friends parents if your going to let your kids stay at the friends house whether it be overnight or just to go over and play. It is very important that parents be home when your child spends time with a friend. I believe if you take care of situations involving your child and their friends, you will be surprised as to how your child will act and behave. It is a good idea to have their friends over to your house occasionally so you can get to know them. Mary and I let our kids have friends over and it worked quite well. The kids had fun and we did not have to worry about what they were doing. I might add that we did have to sit on them occasionally, but it was well worth it. Our kids truly appreciated the way we did things with and for them. Your kids will respond positively if you treat them with love and respect. You might think that your kids will think that you do not trust them but instead they will be glad that you are watching out for them.

Another one is smoking. If mom or dad are smokers, you can almost guarantee that the children will become smokers. This is of course a health hazard to the child as well as those around them because of the secondary smoke. There is not much more to say about this problem because you as parents need to monitor your behavior to help your children.

Being lied to is another problem that children can have. Children want to know the truth and if they cannot get it at home, they will search for it outside of the home. Many times what they get is not the truth and they can get into trouble. When your children ask you a question, you need to tell them the whole truth. There will be times when they ask things that may be hard to answer by being totally truthful, but if your not they will find the real truth somewhere else and they may lose trust in you.

There are several things that can and are commonly called addictions and those are, alcohol, legal and illegal drugs, food, sex and a variety of other things that people, especially children, may end up using and even abusing. Most of this is due to things not going well between them and their parents. These things become a crutch for many people to help them get over the fears and pain that they have or are presently suffering. Most if not all of these problems can be fixed before they occur if you as parents do your job the way God would like for you to. These problems come up when your kids do not get what they need at home. Remember, children know what they need and want from their parents and also know where to get what they need if parents fail to provide them.

A major problem that is continually growing in our society is gangs. It is easier for a gang to recruit members than you might think. Everybody wants to feel loved, accepted and disciplined. This is one of the biggest draws of a gang because they can fill all of those needs. Of course, they will fill them for their own purposes and not your child's. Gangs are causing major problems all over this country. They set rules that each member must follow or else. Would you want your child put into a situation like that? I certainly hope not. Gangs are growing because parents are not taking the proper care of their children. Remember your children are God's children and they are born with a heart of love. They only want to be loved, accepted and disciplined to live a normal happy life.

The things that are listed above are some of the many problems that we unfortunately allow are kids to become a part of whether they want to or not. We as parents need to be aware of the surroundings that our children are in so we can have a better handle on protecting them. Speaking of protecting our children, the best way is, and I have said this several times before is to have a growing relationship with God and your family. Taking time out as individuals and as a family to listen to God, reading His word and spending time in prayer is the best possible answer to life's problems. There again that is a decision that each person needs to make for their own life.

What are we doing wrong as parents to cause the problems that our children are having? Are we at fault? The obvious answer to that question has to be decided by each parent. They must look at how they are raising their children and decide what they might need to change, if anything. I know from personal experience that if we do not raise our kids correctly, they may indeed get themselves into trouble. What that trouble could be is anybody's guess. However, I can guarantee it will not be good for the kids and if you truly love them, it will not be good for you either. We are selling our kids short and hurting them if we do not take the needed time to raise them the way they deserve. Remember, children are a gift of God and should be treated with utmost respect. This will mean to raise them the way God wants you to. In the end, and I speak from experience, it is easier to raise them correctly. If you do, you will find more joy as will your children.

It is my hope and prayer that after reading and absorbing the contents of this book and of course the Bible, that you will be able to use the information to help raise your family. One of the most important things that I can think of is to make sure to listen to your children and help them to make decisions that they need to make. The weekly family meeting and discussions during the rest of the week are vital so that the whole family is on the same page with each other.

We cannot blame our children for getting into the trouble that they do. After all, the parents are sending them on that road to trouble that they are going down. As I have said many times, children need to be loved, accepted and disciplined at home to give them the best opportunity to stay on the right path to adulthood and a good life. Once they reach the age of accountability, which varies with each child, they must be ready to answer for their own actions and life. (NIV 1 Corinthians 13:11)

I pray that you as parents have done your job and if your children have gone out on their own and been successful, you and your spouse can continue your life's goals and feel good about your accomplishments with your children. Prayerfully, they will raise their own children the same way that you raised them. That would be what you would call a 'happy family'

I would like to challenge you to look at the way you handle things with your family. See if you can make changes that will affect the family in a positive manner.

Chapter 15: In Conclusion

It is my hope and prayer that the message in this book will indeed help you to raise your children the way God would want you to. That is the best way a parent can honor God. It also is the best way that you as a parent can honor your children. The scripture mentions some verses that you might want to read and see that God indeed truly loves all of His children. I have enclosed a list of several scriptures that you might want to look up and share with your family. That in itself will show your family that you are on the right road to caring for them. Do you remember that we mentioned the guidebook in Chapter 2? Well, I believe the Bible is "THE GUIDE BOOK", to show us how to raise our children and have a good life. Not all families have the same situation in their homes because people are different and look at things differently; therefore, they need to interpret the information in the Bible according to their families needs. I want to emphasis, that the Bible does not change, but families need to change and adjust their family life to follow what the Bible says. I am convinced that following the Bible can and will help you as parents to not only live your lives as God wants for you, but also to raise your children up in the same way. The rewards far out weigh the problems your kids, and even you as parents, may face unless their raised properly. It comes down to a decision that you and your spouse need to make individually and together.

I want to look at the negatives and the positives of raising children.

Let us look at the positives first since they are the ones that will lead to the best results for you and your family. First, I believe raising your children and living your lives the way that God wants you to will be the most positive direction you can take for your whole family. I do not believe there are any negative ways of raising your children God's way, unless you do not follow His word. That does not mean to say that you will not have problems raising your children according to God's way because, after all children are children. They will be testing you in everyway possible. As we have said before, since you have both agreed to start a family, and you find that you are going to have a baby, you can now put into practice what you have learned since you have been married. Some of these things may seem silly but you will want to be as ready as possible for the blessed event. I have said before that God has a plan for every person who is born. This includes the baby that you will be having. It would be nice if we knew what that plan was, but things just do not work that way. We have to listen to what God is telling us in His word and through prayer to find out what that plan for our child is and for our whole family. He will give us the instructions on raising His child to attain that plan. We just need to be willing to listen and follow.

We have looked at several thoughts and ideas from getting your lifestyle in tune with God, finding the right mate to share your life with and how to take care of the children that you may have. I just want to go over a few things that we have discussed and perhaps clarify some of the points of interest. I want to share with you some final words that will hopefully help you in making the right decisions, in not only yours, but your families lives. After all, life is too short and we need to enjoy it. What is more important for a family than being happy and enjoying life with God? I cannot think of a thing. At least that is the way it is in my family.

Having a positive outlook on life and living a positive lifestyle with your family is what I call true happiness in a world filled with sadness. Even with all the sadness that is around you, you can be happy with the way you have chosen to live and enjoy your family. Remember, we said that the home is the most influential place your child will ever be. If you take care of your family positively, they will be able to ignore the sadness around them much easier, because your children can come home and know they will be safe and loved. You as their parents are their role models and you have the ability to override other role models if you do your job correctly. Children are the most vulnerable to the problems that our society has and unfortunately, it is easier to fall prey to those problems than what one might think. That is why it is extremely important to educate our children about what goes on in society and try not to hide it from them. Treating them in the proper fashion, as we have talked about before, will give them the confidence they will need to help them keep out of the problems that they face every day and could have normally gotten involved in. We should be ready to apologize to any member of the family that we get upset with. This will be good training for everyone in the family. Like we have said, no family will be perfect, but we can all try to be the best person we can be and be the best role model for not only our children but for all those around us.

The main purpose of this book is to try to share from my own family's life and others that I have been involved with on how to live a life that is full of promise and love. In my opinion, raising a family is the best and most enjoyable part of life. Everybody deserves to be happy and to enjoy life to the fullest. This is what God truly wants for us. I believe with all my heart that if we put our faith in God, He will see us through our whole life and help us to get through it all on a daily basis. That does not mean that we will have everything we want, but it does mean that He will take care of our needs. Since God has a plan for each of us, He will surely know what we need and He promises to provide for us. We must trust Him with all our hearts. (NIV Matthew 6:25-34)

We must be realistic and believe that it is a cruel world out there. We can see it on a daily basis. There are things going on that can and will be devastating to us. We have to look beyond what is going on and maintain our faith in God and truly enjoy life the way He wants us to. One very important thing that we should do is to spend time in quality prayer on our own and with the family. Encourage each person in your family to learn to pray and ask God to help them through their day. Believe me it helps more than you can imagine. Remember that God will help you, but you must do your part, follow His word, and be sure to ask for His help. He has given us our choice, so you have to make the choice to follow or not. It is definitely not a free ride. You have to participate and of course be patient.

One more very important item to cover is your children. Like I have said before, children face a tough time in our society today. They deserve the best that life has to offer. After all, they are Gods creation. It is an awesome responsibility to be a parent, but a very rewarding one. I have to believe that parents of children that go to the wayside and get into trouble, have to hurt for them. At least I hope so. No one should enjoy seeing a child in trouble or suffer in any way. These problems can be solved if parents are true to God and to each other and will love their children with all their heart. If this happens, I believe we will solve the majority of the problems we have with our children and society in general.

We talked earlier about the innocence of a child. That innocence can last for several years depending on the child. Anyone who takes that innocence away from a child is one who cannot possibly have the love of God in them. It is important that we teach and treat our children with all the love, acceptance and discipline that we can. We need to keep them out of harms way. That harm can be from alcohol, drugs, sex whether willing or not and many other potential vices that await them if they do not have the love, acceptance and discipline they need at home. That does not mean that everything will be perfect in your home, but it does mean that life will be a lot better and more enjoyable.

Bottom line is, if we can maintain a positive attitude toward our family and love them, accept them and discipline them, and most important of all keep God in the center of our lives, we will stand a greater chance of raising a wonderful family. You must let your children know that they can come to you with any problem, no matter how big or small or that covers any subject. If they know that they can be honest with you without you getting mad at them, you will see that they will come to you more often. This will increase their trust in you and will show them that you do love them and are interested in what they are doing. Believe me it really works. Children need to have the proper information to make the proper decisions for their lives. I truly believe that no child wants to get into trouble. If they are misinformed and have not had the proper up bringing, they will make mistakes and get into trouble even if they do not want to. Rejection of a child in any way by their parents will cause them to rebel because they will believe they are not important or loved. Self-esteem is how a person feels about himself or herself. The better they feel, the higher their self-esteem. Your child's self-esteem is the most important way to measure how well you are doing as a parent. The better you do your job, the better your child's self-esteem will be. This is a very important measuring tool of how a child is doing.

One of the most important things needed in raising your children is that you must know where they are at all times. You also need to know the parents of any close friend of your child's. It is vitally important for your child's sake and for your sanity to know these things. Most of the problems begin with not knowing where your child is and not knowing their friends parents. I know that it worked with Mary and I and I am sure it will work for you. You also need to know about parties that your child may attend. Sometimes these parties can get out of control, especially if you do not know the parents who are giving the party. There are parents who are hosting parties for their children and their friends. They are providing alcohol and some drugs at the party. The logic is that if I let them do drugs or drink at home, they will not have to go looking for it outside. That is definitely a stupid statement. If anything, it can encourage the young people to drink and use drugs elsewhere. First of all, it is illegal and the parents may be arrested and charged with contributing to the delinquency of minors. Bottom line is to be cautious when it comes to your children's activities. You will not be sorry.

I mentioned being truthful with your children earlier in the book. I did want to add that questions that your children ask should be age sensitive. In other words, if your child asks about where do babies come from and they are not at an appropriate age to be specific, then you will need to answer the question to meet the child's needs at that time. That will satisfy their curiosity for the time being. As they mature, you can give an answer that is more specific.

I found, using my own life, that no matter how bad things get, you can count on God to see you through it if you are serious about following His directions. I want to let you know that your life will change with God, but I need to tell you that it will take time and you will need to be patient. It took a lot of time for me to get my life in order, but it was well worth it. The closer you get to God, the more that Satan will attack. If you keep your eyes and heart on God, you will succeed. I believe with all my heart that if you follow God and live your life according to His will, you will have a blessed life. God will take care of your needs if you just ask Him and then let Him. Remember patience is a virtue.

Children have a strong need to be cared for. If their not and their self-esteem goes so far down, they may not care enough for themselves to want to tell anybody or to seek help. This will lead to problems that they may not be able to handle or even want to. I have a granddaughter who has had so many problems in her life that she just does not care. She has a four year old son that she is trying to take care of but has to leave him at a sitters most of the time. She is now twenty years old. She has given indications that she could commit suicide. Her problems began at home and it was due to her mother and father's lack of care for her. Her boyfriend beats her and takes her money. He does not really care about her except for what he can get out of the relationship. One might ask, why stay in this relationship. The reason is the typical one, and that is because her self-esteem is so low that she does not care about herself. She stays because in her mind, he cares for her no matter what he does to her. This is a real example of what can and does happen in our society that people do not realize. This all happened because of lack of care as she was growing up. I believe with all my heart that the only way to correct this and all other problems is to allow God to work in ones life. God created all people equal and He sees no color. In other words, if we follow God, we also should not see color and treat all people the same. God wants us to love everybody but not necessarily like what they do.

I want to express some final thoughts and those are, to emphasize the importance of mom and dad in a child's life. As God is our heavenly father, dads are their children's father. We cannot in any way compare ourselves to God, but as dads, we need to love and raise our children the way God wants us to. If we do not, we are not only cheating God, but also our children and ourselves. We must, in order to change our society, let it begin in our home. Mom is the one who has the nurturing ability as well as many other abilities and is vitally important to raising her children. It takes both a mom and a dad to raise a child. As was said before, children need to vacillate between mom and dad as they are growing up. At different points in their lives, they will need either mom or dad and most times both parents.

I believe one of the most important things that a person can do for another, whether it be a spouse, a friend or a child is to tell them how you feel about them. It takes so little time to tell someone how you feel about them whether saying "I love you", "you're a good friend" or even using the phrase that says to your children "I am so glad that you are my son/ daughter and I love you with all my heart". You would be amazed at what that can do for someone's self-esteem, especially a child. Giving someone a note can make what could be a bad day into a great day. We must not forget that a handshake with a friend or a pat on the head of a child can make a persons day. I would suggest that maybe you can try some of these suggestions and see how they work for you.

I want to make what I think is a very important statement in concluding this book. Parents, if you do the best you possibly can in raising your children and raise them according to God's will, you should never feel guilty about their outcome. If you happen to have a child that has either mental or physical problems love them and care for them with all the love you can give. All children born are God's creation and need to be cared for in the best possible way.

I would like to close with this statement. I pray that you and yours will have a blessed life. The best way that I know of to have that life is to allow God to be involved and share with you. God bless you.

SCRIPTURE REFERENCES:

I have included the following scriptures, from the NIV for you to read and study. It is my prayer that they will be of some value to you.

Love: "God's Love to me"

John 3:16
Romans 5:8
1 John 3:1
1 John 4:8
John 14:30-31
Matthew 6:25-26
Hebrews 13:5
Ephesians 5:1
Ephesians 5:28-30

Acceptance:

Luke 15:11-32
Luke 3:22
Genesis 4:7
Acts 10:35

Discipline:

Proverbs 6:20
Proverbs 22:6

Proverbs 3:12
Proverbs 5:23
Hebrews 5:8
Ephesians 6:1-4
Proverbs 8:32-35
Proverbs 19:18,20

Commitment:
2 Timothy 1:12
Proverbs 31:10-31
Matthew 15:22-28
Psalms 37:5
Matthew 28:20

Encouragement:
1 Samuel 30:6
Matthew 5:3-12
Genesis 28:1,3
Genesis 4:7
Job 11:13-20

Forgiveness/Grace:
Matthew 6:14-15
Matthew 17:3-4
Luke 15:11-32
1 John 2:1-2, 9-13
Romans 5:8

Respect:
2 Chronicles 19:7
Proverbs 28:21
Romans 2:11
Colossians 3:5
James 2:1,9

Acts 10:34
Ephesians 6:1-2
Mark 10:19

Communications:
Genesis 3:8-9
1 Corinthians 15:33
1 Timothy 6:18
Hebrews 13-16
Ephesians 4:29
Colossians 3:8

What Kids Think:
Genesis 3:8-9
Luke 15:11-32
1 Corinthians 13:11
1 Kings 3:7
Proverbs 17:6